I0796795

VELOCITY
PRESS

Holly Dicker is a club culture journalist and independent radio broadcaster with bylines in *the Wire*, *the Guardian*, *Mixmag*, *Electronic Beats*, *DJ Mag* and *Resident Advisor*, where she was a former staff writer. In addition to writing and moderating live talks and panel discussions about nightlife, she is the curator of the Google Arts & Culture multimedia exhibition *A Brief History of Gabber* and producer of the TV documentary *Rotterdam Rave Culture: 30 Years of Heritage* with filmmaker Dennis van Rijswijk. Holly has been a Rotterdammer since 2015, and a raver since 2005.

First published by Velocity Press 2025

velocitypress.uk

Printed and bound in Great Britain by Clays Ltd, Elcograf S.p.A.

Cover design: ST-DUO

Typesetting: Paul Palmer-Edwards

Editor: Duncan Dick

PHYSICAL ISBN: 9781913231859
EBOOK ISBN: 9781913231866

GPSR

Publisher: Velocity Press, London, United Kingdom
EU Authorised Representative: Easy Access System Europe - Mustamäe tee 50, 10621

Tallinn, Estonia, gpsr.requests@easproject.com

CONTENTS

PREFACE: WRITE OR DIE

This diehard anthology has been compiled and revised from over a decade reporting on hardcore as a freelance club culture journalist living between Berlin and Rotterdam. These ideas and anecdotes have been broadcast over multiple talk shows for PRSPCT Radio and my own independent series for Red Light Radio in Amsterdam, between 2018 and 2020.

The rest has been carefully pieced together from interviews and early morning discussions over kitchen tables with artists and fans, multiple heartfelt record and event reviews, as well as several expansive articles published online. The following have served as the springboard for several chapters: *Gabber at 30: Hard, fast, and louder than ever* (*DJ Mag*, October 2023); *The return of Loftgroover* (*DJ Mag*, April 2022); *Tresor at 30: The evolution of a Berlin techno institution* (*DJ Mag*, September 2021); *Pushing back: Women are dismantling the hardcore boys' club* (*Mixmag*, November 2019); *Discover the extreme hardcore-fueled sound of Kilbourne* (*Electronic Beats*, November 2019); *Where were you in '92? An interview with Manu Le Malin* (*Resident Advisor*, January 2019); *Marc Acardipane: The Mover* (*Resident Advisor*, March 2018); *Thunderdome: 25 years of hardcore* (*Resident Advisor*, February 2018); *2017 in electronic music: Hardcore spreads its wings* (uncredited) (*Resident Advisor*, December 2017); *Bang Face: Neo-rave utopia* (*Resident Advisor*, June 2015).

There's also the countless hours clocked shuffling closed-eyed and screwfaced across a vast swathe of temporary autonomous dance-zones, as a hardcore raver since 2005: lost in WWII bunkers, decrepit cinemas with the floor missing, and breweries waiting to be bulldozered, but also football stadiums, party boats and historic nightclubs, plus many many warehouses, in rain and sun and perpetual night, usually until the system shuts off, the lights come up, and sleep is pushed to next week...

This book has had several false starts. Initially pitched on a whim in May 2021, and then again, for real, another covid-amnesia year later. The idea was planted by hardcore researcher and musician Federico Chiari in February 2020, and we did a lot of preparation together. I look forward to reading his definitive history of hardcore, the story of Italian gabber temple Number One has been published online by NERO.

I've avoided the definitive route, choosing instead to ride in convoy behind the trailblazers who embody some of the wider or lesser known ideas about hardcore, what it means, and why it will never die. This is a history of hardcore and not the history of hardcore, because hardcore is so nuanced and personal, my definition of hardcore is not yours, but both our definitions are true, if they are truly felt. This partly explains why *Dance or Die* has taken several years to complete, and why most of it has been dashed off intuitively in the final weeks, after getting totally lost in trying to figure it out.

What does hardcore mean to me? Once I tuned into that, the rest came easily, because this is also my history of hardcore, written through the prism of my own tastes and experiences, especially over the latter chapters, where I am reporting direct from the scuffed concrete dancefloor, bombarded with inflatable rave "toys" or sliding around a sweat-slicked sportshall. And wherever possible, wherever it makes sense in the narrative, I have made a conscious effort to thread the her-stories through the history.

Dance or Die was composed over a four-year breakdown of social norms and geopolitics, where seismic shifts to how we socialise (and dance) together collided with a cascade of personal crises that have become infinitely bound up in this story. Over the course of writing a book about rave culture, I had become increasingly alienated from raving, and despondent over the present-phuture of our scene. Then I went to a party with my hardcore family, danced to some undanceable breakbeat-techno in a damp basement, and suddenly there was hope again.

Dance or Die has been supported by Gemeente Rotterdam and the Private Bank of Grandma. A special thanks to all the editors who believed in me, the friends and family who encouraged me to keep going, to Stefan and Caroline, and all the raves, real and reanimated, that kept me sane through the insanity. To borrow the wise words from a hardcore contemporary (and personal hero): music is awesome consumed alone but best experienced with the ones you love, ideally in the blinding glare of a stroboscope.

Portugal, March 2025

WE HAVE ARRIVED

NIGHT OF THE
RAVERS

1

In an industrial estate in outer Frankfurt, amongst scurrying cockroaches and discarded laundry, a hip hop head in his twenties is ravaged with nightmares. He pours genuine fears for the fate of mankind into his self-built studio, fucking up a drum machine until it kicks out a sound that will raze all previous notions of techno to the ground.

"We came from rap, so we never fitted into that scene," explains Marc Acardipane, the mischievous God of the Godfathers. "One morning I looked in the mirror and said: 'I'm not from Compton, I'm not black, maybe we should find the street sound of Europe.'"

The year was 1990 and hardcore techno had arrived.

Marc Acardipane wanted to be a rockstar. From the age of eight to eighteen he played guitar, taking lessons from his favourite Frankfurt punk group at the time, *Strassenjungs* (Street Boys), the original bad boys of German rock. As a child he used to rent *It's Alive* by the Ramones on cassette from his local bookstore, forming his own punk band in his teens, making unholy noise with a drummer, bass guitarist and singer in a tiny bunker six by six metres wide.

From his Frankfurt bunker youth, Marc pledged to "live for the music or die". But his bandmates were less eager to go all the way. Marc realised he could achieve his dreams with hardware, he just needed a partner as diehard as he was. He met Thorsten Lambart at Cooky's nightclub when they applied there for the same job in 1987. Two years later they formed Planet Core Productions (PCP), the live act and label that would set Marc on his path to stardom.

By 1991 Marc and Thorsten were Frankfurt celebrities: featured on national TV and coverstars of Germany's leading club zine *Frontpage*. They had issued fifteen EPs and two VA compilations via PCP and set up their own distribution company, PCD, the hardest mail order service in the world. They even had their own shop, No Mercy Records, and a Wednesday night residency at one of the best nightclubs in the city.

"We always dreamed, of course, that we will be big," says Marc. But conquering Frankfurt wasn't enough. "Our music is intended for the masses, for everyone, also for the farmers," PCP stated to *Frontpage* in March 1992, as they were about to sign life-changing record deals with major labels Polydor and Sony. "We are not interested whether our records play in clubs or not," they continued. "Our music is not primarily dance music. It's soul music. There is only soul music or soulless music."

Marc knew that this was his destiny from the start. "My friends call me the Mover, because I move things," he explains. Marc was still a waiter at Cooky's when he began making his own style of EBM-meets-Chicago house on borrowed equipment, as Thorsten worked in the warehouse of AMV distributors, learning the tricks of the trade. They were both into US gangsta rap, popularised in Frankfurt by *The American Forces Network (AFN)*, and the ex-GIs still based in the Rhine-Main area.

Marc and Thorsten started performing as Freebase Factory for local hip hop battles, with Thorsten as MC Slam Burt, and collaborating with local rappers like Al Rakhun (René Swain) and the teenage Fast H (Hassan Annouri). Pairing rap and breakbeats with a uniquely dark "phuturistic" kind of techno – a decade ahead of Prodigy's *The Fat Of The Land* – they were deemed "too crazy" by their homegrown hip hop scene, and too techno for Frankfurt techno. For Planet Core Productions they needed a new term to rally behind.

"Everything was called techno," explains Marc. Talla 2XLC claimed the term first with his Technoclub event on Fridays at the Dorian Gray, booking bands like Nitzer Ebb, and the Techno Drome International label, releasing a poppy mix of militant EBM and new beat dance styles, which he dubbed "Aggrepo" or aggressive-positive. But "Frankfurt techno" also included the catchy synth pop of 'Electrica Salsa', Sven Väth's first dance hit as the flamboyant frontman of Organisation For Fun, and the hedonistic acid house that would later define his club, the Omen.

Frankfurt was a party city with some of the best nightclubs and resident DJs in the world. The Studio 54-inspired Dorian Gray discotheque, opened in 1978 inside Frankfurt airport, represented the scene in microcosm. International DJs would fly in and out just to play here, as locals developed their eclectic Sound of Frankfurt style on the club's first-class Richard Long-designed sound system. With two dancefloors and a total capacity of 6,000, it was Germany's largest nightclub, and the first afterhour venue, with open-ended nights that lasted well into Monday.

The PCP duo spent many weekends partying across the border at the Boccaccio in Ghent, epicentre for the kind of dark, druggy dance music that would end up populating the PCP label. But if Belgium had the music, Frankfurt had the rest. Alongside the clubs and the DJs, it was a record industry leader with an enviable infrastructure of shops, global vinyl distributors, professional recording studios and platinum-selling pop producers, as well as a glut of niche and major labels, including Sony's Dance Pool, one of Germany's most successful dance music majors, which headquartered in the city.

Boy Records on the Klingerstrasse and the Delirium Record Store, which opened later on Töngesgasse, were the meeting points for Frankfurt's techno community, where Marc worked every Wednesday morning – not for the money, for the music. "For me it was only important to see the new records, and to play, because I didn't have turntables."

At the entrance to the Dorian Gray was the tiny Air Embargo store, run by skateboarder Mike Hoppe, which sold merch and rave wear as well as records. Mike would be one of the first stockists and supporters of PCP, before joining the crew as a performing member, designer and producer. "I played sometimes in his shop," Marc continues, "so people can buy the records they hear, and everybody was totally on ecstasy."

Marc and Thorsten were well placed to start their own dance music enterprise. But in 1989 they couldn't get a record deal, so they did it themselves: "In Frankfurt we do not follow, we make the trend, you know."

They distributed through "word of mouth propaganda" the first two PCP white labels: *Into Mekong Center* was Marc's first proto-techno record as Mescalinum United. The other was the duo's industrial hip hop EP, *Born To Go*, as Freebase Factory, featuring a moody blue photo of themselves on the cover, their own faces obscured by long black curly wigs – the first of many disguises they'll don.

A flurry of releases followed throughout 1990, including the inaugural *Frankfurt Trax* compilation, *House Of Techno*. This was PCP's battle-response to the landmark 1988 British compilation, *Techno! The New Dance Sound of Detroit*, curated by Neil Rushton together with Derrick May for Virgin imprint 10 Records. The Frankfurters thought they could do it better. Harder.

The *Frankfurt Trax* series was PCP's claim on the emerging techno culture, a way to define it on their own terms, distinct from Detroit's soulful firstwave and from the dominant Europop and EBM sounds of Frankfurt. *House Of Techno* appeared to present a corral of fresh techno talents with exotic names like T-Bone Castro and Tres Hombres, producing a range of paranoid rave music peppered with hip hop and agitated ambient, seemingly united by a shared druggy sci-fi agenda. In fact, these ten tracks were all produced by Marc, with Thorsten as creative co-conspirator, in a five-day delirious recording session typical of the pair.

House Of Techno marked the beginning of PCP's worldbuilding, which would elevate the label to mythological status. The aliases would multiply over the years (totalling more than 80) and develop complex, interrelated backstories. Marc and Thorsten gave each character a mugshot with an Atari computer program used by police – but they really came alive in the media, which PCP courted (and confounded) from the start.

Of the six *Frankfurt Trax* compilations, all but the last had major label distribution. These techno-renegades were signed to Sony's dance music subsidiary, Dance Pool, after Marc stormed the offices one day in a motocross helmet with his latest record, *What Is..? Fick Dich* and a scribbled note to Dance Pool director Stefan Trapp that said: 'Hey Stefan, Fuck You!'

"One week later we had 200,000 DM," Marc laughs. "At that time we lived in a place with no electricity and cockroaches. A couple of weeks later we sit in a 200-square-metre studio with distribution."

But Marc and Thorsten had to fight to be recognised by their own scene. When *Reflections Of 2017* first came out as a white label promo in 1990, it was largely ignored by Frankfurt's DJ elite. It would take a few years – and some outside investment – for the rest of the world to realise what Marc instinctively knew about 'We Have Arrived' when he wrote it. Brooklyn firecracker DJ and seasoned record producer Lenny Dee got it immediately, igniting a transatlantic partnership that turned this Frankfurt hardcore techno sound from local oddity to global phenomenon.

During Mayday Cologne Lenny premiered this dread-filled alien dance music to thousands of twitching, rushing bodies, its doomsday siren cutting through the stadium, as claps popped off like warning shots. "Still to this day I've never seen that many people react all at once to a record," says Lenny. "When Mescalinum United started, that was it. It just ripped the house down."

More significant than the R & S Records showcase that night, which included Mentasm master Joey Beltrum from Queens performing alongside Aphex Twin; Lenny dropping 'We Have Arrived' was a watershed moment, heralding a new chapter for house and techno: "Afterwards, Renaat [Vandepapeliere] says to me, he grabs me and goes: 'Lenny, that shit was hardcore.' I looked at him and I said, 'You know, you're fucking right. I think this is a new fucking style!'"

Marc and Lenny had met by chance sometime in early '91, in a dark and scary Frankfurt warehouse with the chemical stench of amyl nitrate pumping through the smoke machine. Marc "rescued" Lenny from the rain, taking him to the High Pressure Jam Terrortories studio to listen to the first *Frankfurt Trax* series. "It was like destiny," says Lenny. "I was sitting in a room on the floor, smoking pot and fucking going nuts when I first heard these tracks. We made the deal that night."

Lenny was just starting his label, Industrial Strength, when he heard these tracks from Marc. That was it," he says. "I had other tracks ready to go. But I said, I'm gonna push every one of those back. We gotta make this the first Industrial Strength record, and I will play this all over the fucking world."

Two tracks of Marc's most dystopian-sounding techno as Mescalinum United and the Mover launched Lenny's label, rushed to the pressing plant in time for Mayday Cologne.

Uniquely dark and disturbing with something sinister lurking at its core, 'We Have Arrived' would inspire a generation of renegade producers to push techno to the extreme and elevate the distorted kick drum to an (anti-)artform in itself. "'We Have Arrived' revolutionised hardcore," says Lenny. "It had the rave, it had the techno. But it was hard, it was distorted. It got rid of all the happy feelings. Once that record came out, it absolutely changed everything."

Reflections of 2017 – Marc's second EP as Mescalinum United – is one of PCP's most transcendent techno releases; cold, isolated and utterly devoid of human life. The record's titular B-side is just as disturbed and disturbing, with a droning soundscape haunted by ghosts from some imagined nuclear fallout. Both tracks share the nightmare prophecy of a doomed world, translated into sound. The record is so visceral because these visions were real, formed over a series of bleak episodic dreams that plagued the twenty-year-old just before the launch of PCP. Marc explains: "In the morning I was in the future in the dream. I get up and it was completely real, and in the night I follow exactly where I stopped. And it's always playing out the year 2017."

The year 2017 has haunted the PCP output ever since, but pressing Marc for an explanation comes to a dead end. "We're still here," he says, "but it's nothing to do with me or the music, it's the world." He's reluctant to say more because he believes in the power of manifestation – for good and bad: "If I tell you that tomorrow you will have an accident, you will think the whole night on it and then you will have one; if I don't it, you won't. So it's better nobody knows."

In Germany's newly reunified capital, another kind of hardcore techno was forming within a steel and concrete womb five metres underground. On March 13, 1991, Tresor opened in the tomb-like bank vault of the Wertheim Department Store on the Leipziger Strasse, once one of the largest and grandest commercial centres of the 1920s, long since abandoned, and ruinous from war. Close to the "death strip" of the Wall where hundreds died trying to escape the crush of the German Democratic Republic, close to the Führerbunker, where Hitler spent his final demented days, the psychogeography alone made it hardcore from the start.

From these concrete wounds an enthusiastic team cultivated a raw urban utopia, a Berlin in microcosm, building a midnight community from society's outcasts, where musicians and artists, squatters and intellectuals, radicals and punks and anyone else who washed ashore with a willingness to get stuck in found themselves a home, a family, and a dancefloor that would stay open until the last person standing.

Initiated with a short-term rental contract, no official licence, and a structurally unsound building – which the team renovated themselves – Tresor was never intended to last more than a few months. Located on the literal border between East and West, the world's first hardcore techno club was also the first great social experiment of the Reunification. More than two million people from the East crossed over into West Berlin that fateful November weekend in 1989 when the Wall came down, as curious West Berliners began their techno-transformation of the East. Youth from both sides were eager to meet each other, and the city's psychic divisions dissipated in the smoke and stroboscopes. From the lawless and gaping freedom that engulfed Berlin in the early '90s, the city was reclaimed by a generation choosing to dance away the past, stomping over the loss and the uncertainty of the previous decades to forge new destinies for themselves in the dark.

"I think the club was most important for getting people together," says Dadaist and Dreamer Dimitri Hegemann, who co-founded Tresor with Achim Kohlberger when the pair were in their late thirties. Dimitri is the visionary of Tresor, but the organisation was run by women, and powered by its community.

Two eager graduate students ran the club: self-described "team raver" Alexandra Dröner, who managed the bar and bookings, came from the bar of the Fischlabor, the hip Schöneberg hangout predating Tresor, which served hippy homebrew Space beer (which tasted awful) to the bohemian crowd that would become Tresor's hardcore ravers. Fischlabor had open decks in the corner, where Berlin's future DJ talents Tanith and Ellen Allien first tested out their respective techno sounds.

After heading up the building's renovation, Regina Baer became Tresor's managing director, and spent most days on site during its fourteen years on the Leipziger Strasse. One blonde with glasses, the other brunette, both smokers and always laughing – even while mopping up the flooded toilets for the hundredth time – Alex and Regina brought warmth to these long, dark and bitterly cold winter nights.

When Tresor club opened that Spring of '91, the Globus floor was just a bar with a boombox and the subterranean Vault was hidden from sight. Not everyone who visited could even find it at first, which added to the mystery. People drinking in Globus bar would suddenly be accosted by steaming bodies emerging from a slit in the wall at the back. Entering this basement was like stepping into another world, totally isolated from the one above. It was damp and airless, dissected into a dancefloor and bar area by rusted iron railings that glittered in the lasers. The walls were lined with ancient safety deposit boxes that rattled their own tune to the bassy Bose 3028 sound system that was later installed.

In this dungeon crucible, with brutal sounds reflecting off brutalist surroundings, hardcore arrived in Berlin. "The hardness of the steel reinforced walls, the concrete floor, the metal safes and gate, this hardness is what made the Tresor sound," explains Regina Baer in *True Stories*. It wasn't just the sound, the entire culture of Tresor was hardcore, from the intense working conditions imposed on its staff, the inhospitable bunker environment, to the dance or die demands of its dancefloor, where only the true techno warriors would survive.

"You will have a hard time finding people smiling ecstatically or on a mission to find themselves," wrote Klaus Mayer in his 1991 review of the club for the Berlin daily *TAZ*. "In here the beat is fired into your stomach so that you have to move, whether you want to or not. This is Techno..."

"Working downstairs in the Vault was hardcore," admits original bar staffer Susanne Deeken in *True Stories*, who worked open-ended bar shifts inside a metal cage, standing in ten centimetres of water, with just the blinding flash of a strobe for light. "But the people were so super happy and friendly, full of love, almost hippies," she adds.

"It was hard everywhere. Even the afterparties at der Walfisch were hard," says Tanith about the infamous after hours club on the corner of Köpenicker Strasse that opened up during Berlin's techno-boom, where sexworkers and punks mingled with the hardcore techno hedonists behind taped up windows. "Everything was hard at that time because it fitted perfectly with the Wall coming down and the vibe of the city," says Tanith.

Tanith moved to West Berlin in 1986, chasing the industrial music scene he'd been playing and promoting in youth clubs in his hometown of Wiesbaden – where the rich Frankfurter bankers lived, says Tanith. He hated the vibe of Frankfurt, with its social divisions and hierarchies. Tanith fully embraced the egalitarian power of Berlin techno and the anonymity of the Tresor basement, where egos and identities gave way to the shadows.

Down here the DJ was just a DJ, and in between sets they're on the dancefloor raving. "I never thought DJing would determine my life or something," says Berlin's first and longest-serving techno DJ. "I had no plans ever. I'm not a person with goals. I just fell into it and then the snowball turned into an avalanche."

Tresor turned this industrial cyberpunk into *Der Bestrafer*: The Punisher, who rallied Berlin's first hardcore generation to dance, arms out, legs planted wide apart beneath his Marvel skull mascot, to commit themselves to the night, and to partying all weekend long. He was the Master of Nasty Sounds, who wore military clothing as a provocative statement against the house elite who damned him and his music. But Tanith wasn't aggressive, and being the hardest or the baddest didn't interest him; he was a raver, first and always: "If I had wanted to stay tough, I would still play Laibach or Revolting Cocks," he explained to *Frontpage* in 1995.

For Tanith, being invested in the music was important above all. "Some people wanted techno to be open for everyone, but I was like, no, first you have to prove that you dig it," he says. To be *hartcore*, you had to be hardcore for the music too. Hardness had nothing to do with it. "Heaviness is not one-dimensional," he said in an earlier interview with *Frontpage* from '92, as he was moving into breakbeats and a breezier afterhour sound. "If I have softer passages in my set today, it's always because they are new in combination with hardcore. The harder elements violate the softer ones, there are always rough edges. It's just heaviness with different means."

'Blah Blah Soft Blah Blah Blah Hart Blah Blah Breakbeat Blah Blah Blah Hartcore Blah Blah Blah Blah Blah...' ran the flyer for one of Tanith's last Friday night residencies at Tresor, held on August 21, 1992, before taking a break from the basement and his Punisher persona, and all the "blah blah blah" in the Berlin scene that was starting to break off into tribes.

Frontpage magazine syphoned the mood with their end of year issue and its attention-grabbing cover headline: Techno where will you go? "In 1992, the whole thing split, musically speaking," says *Frontpage* editor Jürgen Laarmann in *Der Klang Der Familie: Berlin, Techno and the Fall of the Wall.* "Some wanted it harder, others more melodic."

From 1992 the Berlin techno family was cleaved into enemy camps. One side advocated for even bigger raves, more commercial sponsorship and a poppier, chart-friendly sound. The other violently rejected all that for more subversive, anarchic and diehard modes of expression. This latter camp of Bunker Youths demanded a harsher, louder, more hardcore kind of techno to dance into oblivion. From this moment on, the hardness of Tanith and Tresor would be redefined by the next generation – the black sheep of Berlin techno – who wore boots and hoodies and military gear, and coalesced in the city's dwindling squatted venues, making one last stand against a city about to clean up, sell up and sell out.

INDUSTRY DESTROYERS

Music for your ass

HARD WAX

progressive dance music

U.S.A.

vacuum tube/vicious acid
w p a kamikaze (UR)
w p a the seawolf (UR)
w p a belgian resistance (UR)
maurizio ploy
der klang der familie (transmat)
q - bik muz kinetic motion
nude photo remix (white label)
fade to black insync remix (white label)
blake baxter fuck you up remix (white label)
n2o e.p.
underground resistance world to world
nick holder digital age
proteus 1 poison
paul johnson in the kitchen
yello bostich hardcore remixes
rhythm in style just go
dark comedy war of the worlds (white label)
fuse flexi disc + comic

t - shirts :

transmat (long sleeves)
UR
+ 8
made in detroit
KMS
happy
strictly rhythm
probe
moby
maurizio
eight ball
punisher

caps :

transmat
UR
+ 8

DJ-HOTLINE:
MO-FR 12-18.30
SA 10-14 UHR
BERLIN 618 88 46

U.K.

rabbit city 6
edge 3
fresh vegetables
mind over rhythm the crossing
cats & whiskas e.p.
x - certificate rising to the bass
love e.p. (E)
s.l.m. now it's finished
wax doctor basement promo
midsummer madness e.p.
nightbreed native breed
the men from del bosca
alienation e.p. 3rd party
B 12 redcell e.p.
system 7 altitude (mayday mix)
caustic window joyrex j4, j5
underground resistance revolution for change compilation
reload 3

EURO

yennek
lenny dee
edge of motion
art 1
dj hell
t.o. 001
psyche crackdown remix
r&s lila mescalinum united/aphex twin
terrace
problem house
pelgrim
sperminator

LADEN & VERSAND

LISTE ANFORDERN !

REICHENBERGER STR. 75
1000 BERLIN 36

2

In a turreted hospital-squat on the Mariannenplatz a mysterious multiracial band from Detroit closes Berlin's first fully electronic dance music festival. Their industrial hip hop clangs a new rhythm from the silent machine halls of the Packard Plant. A post-punk music journalist – the "secretary" – is charged with looking after the group, which includes a certain Wizard on synths. Nobody in Berlin knows he is also a Punisher behind the decks, and one of Detroit's most highly skilled radio disc jockeys.

Back in Motor City, two pissed off musicians became three, faceless and standing in for the many, to wield techno like a sledgehammer – to break up the system, and then rebuild something better; a real community, where Detroiters look after Detroit. Tired of seeing their brothers exploited, this techno militia were going to take charge of their own destinies, bypassing the authorities that had failed them again and again, to rap with keyboards and drum machine a new kind of techno-message, radical, soulful, full of hope for the future. Their sound was militant, their manifesto confrontational: "We make no compromises. We can't be controlled. We take control!"

"Maybe Detroit was economically depressed, but musically richer than a mothafucker," says "Mad" Mike Banks in the documentary, *Somewhere in Detroit*. "My arch enemy: major record companies and their need for greed. They kill culture, man."

Underground Resistance was just that: a DIY techno movement

against commercialism and individualism, founded by Banks and Mills in 1989. Banks started in a rock group before forming the jackin house band Members of the House, which paved the route to Underground Resistance – in setup, if not in sound. Mills, meanwhile, had spent the '80s learning his craft by sneaking into clubs, underage, to watch his elder brother's crew of DJs perform, and mixing his own three-to-five-hour radio shows every night for eight years on WJLB radio.

They had both been burned by the majors. "I had a really bad time with Final Cut," Mills told journalist Frank Broughton in 2005, "we had to literally give our music away to get out of bad contracts. It was really ridiculous. I thought, if I'm going to make a career out of the music industry, I'm going to basically have to do everything myself."

The pair officially met during the recording of Mills' Final Cut album, *Deep In 2 The Cut* – the record that Dimitri Hegeman would discover during a trip to Chicago, rummaging through a bucket of rejected demos at Wax Trax! Records. Dimitri signed it to his Big Sex label, and booked Mills to play with the band at Atonal Festival in March 1990 – his first (of many) visits to the post-war ruins of Berlin.

Dimitri's Atonal Festival was at the forefront of Berlin's experimental art and music scenes, booking British industrial bands like Psychic TV, Test Dept. and Bourbonese Qualk and provocative performance groups like Einstürzende Neubauten and Sprung aus den Wolken from the homegrown *Geniale Dilletanten* (Ingenious Dilletants) movement. But by 1990's fourth (and final founding) edition, Atonal ditched the guitar-orientated music of the past for this acid house dance phenomenon from Britain and Manchester's mythical Haçienda. Madchester acts Cosmic Baby, 808 State and Baby Ford were billed alongside a "continuous dance party" hosted by DJ Mike Pickering, with the sophisticated computer music of Clock DVA headlining the first day, and Final Cut billed – unannounced – for the close.

"We made them sleep on the floor," admits Carola Stoiber in *True*

Stories. Carola would eventually manage the most influential techno label in the world, but at this moment she was just the secretary and facilitator of Dimitri's Interfishing in outer space schemes. She was still studying to be a journalist, and busy blazing her own trail. With her deep raspy smoker's voice, cropped blond hair and big nerdy glasses, she came across more austere than she was at heart. Carola took no shit from nobody – but cared deeply for everybody, including Mills and the band when they arrived, shivering, to a Berlin still waking from its winter deepfreeze. "I drove the guys around in my old Citroën and brought them some blankets," she recalls in *True Stories*. "We also checked out the UFO with the band, Tresor hadn't opened yet."

This pattern would repeat over Carola's two decades as Tresor Records manager, which saw her forge meaningful connections with her roster over late night chats at the Globus bar and visiting artists in their home environments in Detroit, and later Birmingham, Glasgow and London. "It's important to see how artists live, their surroundings, to understand them better, which I did more often," she says. "You also have to like each other, have the same vision and goals. You cannot just put out a record."

Tresor Records wouldn't exist if Carola hadn't lobbied to be sent to New York City to hunt for new DJ talents during the New Music Seminar, once Tresor did finally open those steel doors to the world. During a networking panel at the Marriott Marquis hotel on Times Square, she was passed a note through the rows of seats. "Hey, I know you from Berlin," it said. It was Jeff Mills, armed with a test-pressing of *X-101*.

The Underground Resistance collective had been attending the New Music Seminar since 1990, and this was their second trip to the Big Apple to spread the new techno-message from the Motor City. The extended crew piled into Banks' work van to make the ten hour drive to America's biggest pop industry meet at the time, dressed in white propaganda t-shirts – designed to turn heads, but not to give answers, because the music had to speak for itself.

Over the weekend Mills DJed at the Limelight, the wildest of the wild Manhattan clubs of the rave era. Made infamous in the 80s with its queer Club Kids subculture, by the '90s this deconsecrated brownstone church on the corner of Sixth Avenue had become a hotspot for celebrities, tourists and raving outer borough youth to party beneath women dancing in cages suspended from its enclaved ceiling. "At the end of the night, Jeff and [UR friend Big] White were offered jobs, and Jeff didn't come home with us," recalls UR member Mike "Agent X" Clark to *Red Bull Music Academy Daily*.

Back in Berlin, summer slipped into Autumn and Tresor kicked up a gear, promoting its new label and release – *X-101* – featuring the deadly groove of 'Sonic Destroyer', a track that had you singing along as you suited up for battle. "That song was to rip off the head of any DJ in front of Jeff, 'cause they would always try to out-spin him, so it was to destroy the DJ," Mike explained in a Tresor-themed *Red Bull Music Academy* lecture.

Underground Resistance toured through Germany and Holland in '91, blowing up the RoXY in Amsterdam, and literally destroying the Tresor basement in Berlin in October – a show that rendered the new Berlin techno crowd motionless with awe, and converted any techno-doubters fully to the cause. "At the end of the Underground Resistance show, nothing worked anymore. Everything was cracked out. The entire system was broken," Dimtri recalls in *Der Klang*. "The performance was a pivotal moment. It was so loud and such a narcotic, everyone just stood there, completely fascinated. You couldn't see anything either, a bomb of sound and smoke went off and blew everything away."

Banks manned the rhythms with keyboards and the 909 whilst Mills handled the decks like a man possessed, flawlessly mixing in a new record every 30 seconds and tossing discarded ones behind him. MC "Rob Noise" Hood assumed the voice of his suffering community. "So it was sort of Public

Enemy with electronics," he says in *Der Klang*. "That militant, subterranean, underground, take-no-prisoners attitude. We were all about struggle."

Like Chuck D and his crew of politicised Long Island rappers, Underground Resistance were weaponsing their music, turning decades of racial discrimination, violence and neglect into a sonic call of action to fight the power – or to 'Riot', 'Rage' and 'Assault' as per their *Riot EP*, which they self-released just ahead of the group's Tresor club debut. "We were coming from Detroit after the riots, after Martin Luther King Jr. was killed," Hood continues in *Der Klang*. "We were living in a city that was slowly dying. A slowly decaying city, a place like no other on planet Earth."

Dressed in the UR uniform, the now iconic black and white UR shirts and black ski masks, they were just three pairs of eyes and hands glinting and thrashing about in the dark. This was truly a pivotal moment for Tresor, marking a sonic shift away from a spacey kind of techno, based on fantasy, into a more brutal techno-realism more suited to the ruinous and liberating cauldron of techno's (re)birth.

UR assumed the urgency and uncertainty of the times, in Berlin and Detroit. Their music responded to the decades of socio-economic decline at home, triggered in the '70s by the Motor City's declining monopolistic car industry, the assassination of Martin Luther King Jr., and the violent race riots of '67 that had left deep psychic scars. If Detroit was going to change, change was going to come from the ground up, by the people of Detroit working together to rebuild, reseed, and reinspire themselves.

That ethos resonated in Berlin, a city previously cleaved in two, with one side forgotten and mismanaged under Allied rule, the other stringently controlled. Reunification euphoria ebbed into crisis more quickly than anticipated, as mass unemployment, poverty and economic uncertainty ripped through Germany through the '90s. When UR arrived in Berlin (one year into the Reunification), nearby Potsdamer Platz was still a no-man's land, littered with rubble, spent bullets and twisted metal sculptures where the exiled "Lost Tribe" of the Mutoid Waste Company lived in squatted trucks. Berlin was an urban playground, up for grabs by those willing to seize these vacant spaces – before the capitalists moved in. And behind every crumbling facade was the potential for a party.

X-101 finally came out in December '91 via a dual-licensing deal that launched Tresor Records in Berlin and Novamute in London. Now with a pioneering club-label dynamic, Tresor could facilitate a unique relationship between techno's growing community of artists and fanbase. Label acts could test out ideas directly on the dancefloor; DJs booked for the club would be signed to the label; and profits from club entrance and drink sales would go straight into advances for new Tresor records. The Tresor club was the ideal promo for new releases, with Carola Stoiber at the helm, supported by Marc Snow working in A&R.

Six months after *X-101* detonated, UR were back at the New Music Seminar for another series of shows at the Limelight. For Disco 2000 on Wednesday, UR member Blake Baxter joined resident Keoki and NYC-Amsterdammers Fierce Ruling Diva, as the Underground Resistance trio headlined Friday's Future Shock night. "This is what you have been waiting for: 100% hardcore!" bellows the MC over a morose and bleepy opening tribute to Detroit techno's innovators Juan Atkins, Derrick May, and Kevin Saunderson (who all played the night before) before UR's battle hit 'Sonic Destroyer' rips through the system. This was the night Mills accepted his career-defining DJ residency at Manhattan's premier rave club.

Shortly after UR's first Tresor Records tour, Mills and Hood left UR to pursue solo careers: Mills moved to New York, and continued touring the hardcore rave scene as it exploded throughout Europe, launching his Axis label together with Hood (still based in Detroit) producing more subtle strains of techno as antithesis to the high-intensity parties Mills was playing most weekends. The *Tranquilizer EP* is the duo's aptly named Axis debut from '92, transforming early Chicago acid house into a flexible, multi-purpose-style of techno: which could be sped up into a banger, or kept slow and softer for late night listening. They simultaneously remained loyal to Tresor, releasing iconic solo debut albums: Mills' *Waveform Transmission Vol. 1*, featuring the caustic techno-delirium 'Berlin' in homage to the city that started it all; and Hood's landmark minimal album, *Internal Empire* from '94.

Tresor Records provided artists the freedom and tools needed to craft their own sound and audience over follow-up records. UR's next album release as X-102, *Discovers The Rings Of Saturn,* was inspired by the group's formative experiences in Berlin, and signed blind by Carola in '92. "They called me, the DAT is here, and when we listened to it, it sounded like everything was backwards," she recalls. "We bought the cat in the bag." With each track referring to a moon or ring of Saturn – in title and track length – it's a sublime and celestial piece of techno.

UR were Tresor's gateway to Detroit, and for the first half of the '90s, Tresor Records was almost exclusively a platform for the city's rich seam of talent, with timeless releases from Juan Atkins, Eddie "Flashin" Fowlkes and Terrence Dixon, as well as Blake Baxter, The Prince of Techno, who accompanied UR to Berlin in '91, and remained in the city to become one of the club's first Detroit resident DJs. It's a testament to Carola's caring and considered approach to signing records, and the trust the people of Detroit placed in Tresor. "We always said we need to build relationships that were long-lasting," says Carola.

Moritz von Oswald, Mark Ernestus and the Hard Wax record store were key in brokering Tresor's defining Berlin-Detroit axis. The Basic Channel duo had already established connections with Detroit, and recommended Detroit DJs to play Tresor when the club first opened; when they did, they stayed at Ernestus' flat.

Over the decade Tresor would add new axes and techno waves to its label-club roster, from the Scottish Sativa collective and Brighton's No

Future crew, Downwards in Birmingham and Blueprint in London, to Japan. But the label's vision has always been the same: "To put out quality techno," says Carola, "and always be a bit ahead of whatever was coming next."

Banks stayed true to his original grassroots mission, of growing and supporting the city of Detroit. Together with Christa Robinson, he launched Submerge Distribution in 1992 as a network for Detroit labels, including Kevin Saunderson's KMS imprint, and the Underground Resistance label, which continued to expand anonymously with the next generation of Detroit techno militia (managed by Cornelius Harris). Submerge doubled as an appointment-only record store located in a claustrophobic bunker on 3000 E Grand Blvd, its walls and ceiling signed by those who have made this hallowed techno-pilgrimage over the years, as a literal realisation of Detroit claiming ownership of their music, their heritage, and collective future.

"Sometimes you would go too far forward and can't nobody catch up," says Banks in *Somewhere in Detroit*, "like with Drex[ciya] it was four, five years before anybody figured out what had happened but I knew this shit was bad as hell, so you just leave it there like a landmine, just leave it there, somebody step on it sooner or later."

In Frankfurt, PCP shared UR's future gaze – but instead of feeling hopeful, they were filled with dread. They needed to prepare their youth for what's coming, with hardcore techno. "Punk was too destructive," Marc explained in PCP's first German TV interview, sitting cross-legged on the floor of their High Pressure Jam Terrortories studio. "Techno is somehow a different message. More for the future. To prepare us for the future."

In the early '90s Frankfurt was one of the most dangerous cities in Germany. Outlaw motorcycle gangs infiltrated its bustling nightlife scene, and shootings, stabbings and violence regularly erupted in and around the city's clubs.

Just like UR, PCP became the faceless front of their own urban dystopia, but instead of black ski masks of anonymity, their crew donned masks of horror and skulked about the stage with bullhorns and flashlights as the hardest Frankfurt Street Boys of the emergent rave scene. "You can ruin yourself here, but that Hardness you face makes you tougher than you were before," explained PCP rapper Radical R to *Frontpage* in March 1992. "Somewhere, the sound is also frustration: that frustrated feeling [that] what you're doing, this city hates."

By 1992 PCP were inciting their hardcore followers to riot with gangsta-indebted hits from their No Mercy Records label. These included '9 Is A Classic', paying tongue-in-cheek tribute to the 9 mm, the gangster's weapon of choice, as Ace The Space, and 'Konstablerwache' about a renowned Frankfurt station where you could reputedly pick up drugs, rapped by their dealer-imitating Moroccan MC Fast H. The crew all had shaven heads, and dressed in matching PCP-brand bomber jackets – their own outlaw gang – as Mike Hoppe skulked about the stage with a gas gun, shooting blanks into the air whenever Marc dropped '9 Is A Classic'.

"Think about doing that today in the club," says Marc. "Back then it was no problem." Their shows were getting increasingly violent, too. "As my MC always says, we can make them fight, cry, love, everything." The end of the world was coming, and PCP wanted their acolytes to be ready. PCP's original message was to teach people the hard feeling "because we know the world get fucked," says Marc, "and if you show people the feeling, with the music, it's a little bit easier."

Mayday 1993 was Judgement Day, when simmering rivalries boiled over into all out turntable-war at Dortmund's Westfalenhalle stadium. Mayday had grown from a scrappy Berlin event with Olympian aspirations into one of the most crucial platforms for international rave culture. Mayday curated all the best talents into ambitious lineups over biannual events, exported to other Germany cities, like Dortmund and Cologne on May Day proper; with the winter edition remaining at its Halle Weissensee home in Berlin.

Mayday flirted with hardcore through the first half of the '90s – because hardcore rave was too big to ignore – but these were reluctant bookings by an organisation interested in pushing more pop-friendly strains of house and techno. "By '92 they already were in the mode: 'we have to control where this thing is going,'" says Tanith, Mayday resident since the inaugural Best of House and Techno edition, held on December 14, 1991. Tanith admits the first Mayday was great, but then fell victim to "too much money and too many egos involved."

All the live acts were given just fifteen minutes to perform. Accompanied by dancers, with the crew dressed all in white and armed with bullhorns, PCP were billed between Mayday's resident DJs Marusha and co-founder DJ Dick. After a long, demented drum machine build up from Marc manning the mixing desk, teasing into the opening lines of their first track – '9 Is A Classic' – they were cut off; their allotted time over. "We started a fight on the stage," says Marc. "One guy flew from five metres into the crowd!" To this day he believes their set was sabotaged, along with others that night: "For Lenny they put up the high frequencies," he says; "for Moby they cut the sound, he threw his keyboard on the floor, he was so pissed."

"Frankfurt and Berlin were enemies. Maybe from Mayday," says Marc, "Mayday was really commercial and they tried to push their DJs, which for us was not real techno."

Lenny returned to Frankfurt with Marc, straight to High Pressure Jam Terrortories studio to unleash their fury into the Leathernecks disstrack 'At War' featuring Lenny screaming pure bile down the mic: "Low Spirit, SUCK MY COCK!" Powered by a bludgeoning Rotterdam gabber kick, 'At War' was included on the fourth *Frankfurt Trax* compilation, *The Hall*

Of Fame, and became a massive hit, thanks to the Sony major label deal. It was the beginning of Lenny and PCP's bald-headed alliance with the flicking and chopping masses gathering in sports halls and convention centres throughout the Netherlands.

MONDAY FEBRUARY 17th 1992
FROM 23.00 TILL 04.00

RoXY PRESENTS

UNDERGROUND RESISTANCE

A COMBINED LIVE / DJ PERFORMANCE
JEFF 'THE WIZZARD' MILLS / MICHAEL BANKS
ALSO STARRING DJ DIMITRI
TICKETS ƒ15.00 IN ADVANCE
AVAILABLE AT THE RoXY

!THIS IS TECHNO!

RoXY, SINGEL 465 AMSTERDAM, PHONE (020)6200354, FAX (020)6269454

BERLIN, GERMANY 91

MAKE SOME FUCKIN NOISE

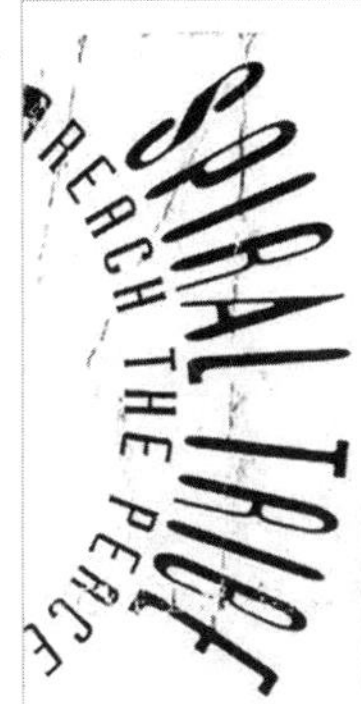

I AM A SAVAGE AND I DO NOT UNDERSTAND
HOW THE BEAUTY OF THE EARTH CAN BE SOLD BACK TO MAN

WEVE GOTTA BATTLE WITH A FORCE THATS BEEN KEEPING US DOWN
TAKE A KEENER LOOK AT WHATS GOING ON AROUND
DONT ACCEPT THAT YOUR VOTE WONT BE COUNTED
COS THE GOVERNMENT RULE AND AFFECT CANT LAST
WHEN WERE LIVING IN THE MOMENT AND NOT HANGING ON THE PAST
SO RESPECT TO THE HARDCORE MOTHER EARTH
AS THIS GENERATION FIND AWARENESS AND WORTH
IN A PLANET THATS BEEN DRAINED OF ITS NATURAL RESOURCES
NOW IS THE TIME TO PICK UP THE PIECES
TO RE-CONNECT AND BLOW FAULTY FUSES.

BREACH THE PEACE BREAK THE BARRIERS MAKE SOME FUCKIN NOISE

SP 23

SPIRAL TRIBE "BREACH THE PEACE" T-SHIRTS AVAILABLE BY MAIL-ORDER.

FRONT: "BREACH THE PEACE" LOGO ETC.
BACK: "MAKE SOME FUCKIN NOISE" SAME TYPE.
SLEEVES: "IN THE AREA" SAME TYPE.

PRINTED BLACK ON GREY. HANES SHORT SLEEVE X-LARGE ONLY.
ALL PROCEEDS GO TO THE SPIRAL TRIBE DEFENCE FUND
PLEASE SEND CHEQUE OR POSTAL ORDER ONLY, TOGETHER WITH DELIVERY
ADDRESS AND RELEVANT BAND DETAILS TO: "S-IRAL-23"

WEST END LANE, WEST HAMPSTEAD, LONDON

PLEASE ALLOW 21 DAYS FOR DELIVERY.

SPIRAL TRIBE
BREACH THE PEACE
ILLEGAL MUSIC IN THE AREA
E.P. OUT 3.8.92

DEFEND YOUR HUMAN RIGHT TO PARTY. THE GOVERNMENT ARE CLAMPING DOWN ON YOUR FUTURE. TAKE ACTION, IT'S YOUR PLANET - YOU KNOW THAT. BE THERE, MAKE SOME NOISE.

FREE PARTY ★ FREE PEOPLE ★ FREE FUTURE

9.45 AM. TUES. 21st JULY 92.
MALVERN MAGISTRATES COURT, WORCESTERSHIRE.

THIS EVENT WILL BE TELEVISED - MAKE THE MOST OF IT.

3

"Right, listen up revellers. It's happening now and for the rest of the weekend, so get yourself out of the house and on to Castlemorton Common... Be there, all weekend, hardcore."

From the big tops of the licensed megaraves, to partying in grimy protest with the rebel-hardcore, or losing it on a Wednesday night with a few hundred people still going from the weekend – or just getting started; as the '90s dawned Britain was going nut nut totally mental ardkore!

"Hardcore means different things to different people, and they're all correct," explains Jason Warlock, who experienced the decade change as a university fresher from the rattling roofs and dirty floors of the booming Hackney Wick warehouse scene. "But in the original days, you would just say 'hardcore' and everyone knew what you meant: hardcore raves being mad, as in, people really losing it in there."

1990 was the flashpoint. Between "fluffy" house music sound systems Tonka and DiY supplying the inaugural "succession of repetitive beats" in the unfenced travelers field of Glasto over three sunny days in June, to Britian's first attempts to curb and criminalise this free party movement five months later, a rebellious hardcore of the ardkore movement formed between sound system crews railing against the criminality, the fines and the raving injustice, with fucking noise!

From these "nosebleed" zealots, who lived hard and played harder, a band of black-clad, shaven-headed tekno-monks rose up and multiplied. Their mission: find the exit and keep on going, pushing the boundaries of sound and sanity, as a community. They were the People's Sound System, because anyone could join, and the Merry Pranksters of ardkore from the spring of '91, when they piled into a van with a rig and a party map from the travellers to embark on their first breakbeat-driven route through the wilds of England.

Only here, rolling through the grassy greens, beneath rosy dawns and twinkling nights were they truly free. They accepted the mission would be a nomadic one, and a rave movement literally facilitated through movement, under stars, not surveillance, out in the fields and forest canopies of Britain's receding common land. As this anarchic splinter of ardkore moved through the unmanned spaces of a country deep in devastating recession – officially the longest since the Second World War by John Major's '92 election, partying free from club restrictions (and entry fees) was not just a whim, but a necessity. "House repossessions continued (75,000 of them in the previous year), unemployment was still rising, the amount owed in consumer credit was twice the level of a decade earlier, and 1,200 businesses were going bust every week," as historian Alwyn W. Turner writes in *A Classless Society: Britain in the 1990s.* Many chose squatting as an alternative, or life on the road, fully liberated from society's constructs.

This subversive existence hardened these hardcore nomads, living a life defined by sleeplessness and survival, and partying as a mode of resistance. They were dependent on raves as a source of income, to pay for petrol, to eat, to live; and they had to rely on each other, as a network of individuals shrugging off the consumerism and self-serving ideology of the 80s to plunge wide-eyed into the void. Some of these people were already involved in the club scene; others just shared the crew's enthusiasm to party and were already living outside the law. Anonymous, anti-hierarchical, hedonistic and flawed, it was a hardcore life and a life lived for hardcore. After that inaugural '91 trip, these Merry Pranksters never felt at home between bricks, or safe under government rules again. They were the Spiral Tribe, hardcore's original outlaws, who took on the government and won, but broke apart along the way.

The original Tribe formed from a group of friends squatting in West London. Painter and decorator Debbie Griffith together with Mark Angelo Harrison (both in their late twenties) would shape the aesthetics of the crew. Mark designed their iconic grinning logo, and all Spiral Tribe events involved an artistic direction – from flyers to immersive decor. Youngest member Simone Trevelyan joined from the first party, held in an old Edwardian school, the Skool House, which they squatted after the magic and violence of Glasto – which ended in a riot between the travellers and security – and the Entertainments (Increased Penalties) Act (the Bright Bill) becoming law. Mark's brother Zander, a tree surgeon, completed the Spiral core, which would proliferate with performers and production crew, revellers and travellers, and anyone else who wished to follow them on their ceaseless party-protest through the '90s.

The Spirals were battling with authorities from the off. Police raided their first De-tension party at the Skool House in October 1990 and confiscated their sound system; Simone supplied the backup, as she worked in a store that hired disco equipment. She helped to create the crew's fledgling rig – once they'd raised enough money (from parties) to buy one. As "Sim Simmer" she became one of the crew's principal MCs and lyricist behind their '92 breakthrough EPs, as tension mounted between the Tribe and police.

The DJs included "Ixy" Ixindamix, a traveller who lived on the road with a horse and cart. She played a significant role in the Tribe's first sound system journey across the English countryside, feeling the seasons change and immersed in this outlaw life that would become their own, between the spring equinox and summer solstice of '91. Ixy would trade her horses for records to join the Spiral convoy as it rolled towards a crisis that would change Britain – and the raving world – forever.

But first, Spiral Tribe together with Circus Normal closed out the year from the derelict ruins of the Roundhouse theatre in Camden. It was a night of triumphs, failures, and new beginnings. The entrance was blocked with a mountain of insurmountable rubble, which the Normals plowed over in their Militant six-by-six-wheel-drive, previously belonging to the Moscow State Circus – with rig and genny onboard. The place was packed, but the DJs couldn't get the system working. The main technician had been rushed to hospital with suspected blood poisoning (or had taken too much speed, depending on sources), and nobody knew how to fix it. With no music and tension mounting between twitchy ravers, police and security, just before midnight, the generator then failed, plunging the Roundhouse into deep and fear-filled darkness, as the people kept piling in. Eventually hot wired to an outside street lamp, the party kicked back up again and lasted until the street lights blinked off at sunrise.

From the revenue of this troubled NYE, the crew launched their first fully autonomous record label. But how were they going to honour the collective spirit of these parties, where everybody was as vital for the rave as each other? "It was important for us to keep the record anonymous for the simple reason that so many people behind the scenes had worked hard to bring the project into being," as Mark writes in his memoir, *A Darker Electricity*. "Spiral Tribe had evolved as a synergetic community. Living by the code of anonymity, we rejected top-down hierarchies and actively created other ways of working together. Some were more successful than others."

This first record was distributed at free parties by the crew themselves, but none of the money from sales came back to the label, or collective, and most of the records were confiscated by police. With the last of the Tribe's dwindling funds, they recorded their next release, *Breach The Peace* (with lyrics written and performed by "Sim Simmer" Simone). Using industry connections from Spiral Tribe member Lol Hammond, *Breach The Peace* was picked up by Martin Glover (AKA Youth from Killing Joke) at Big Life, at the time releasing acts like The Orb, Coldcut and De La Soul. This major label and multi-record deal came with a massive cash advance – arriving just as the Tribe were about to embark on the longest and most expensive legal trial in British history.

"In a tiny bedroom studio, somewhere in the heart of Romford, a computer screen flickers into life. In a few more hours, the final mix of yet another homemade hardcore white label will be in the can. Two weeks later it will be pumping out of the pirate airways and the finished vinyl flying out of specialist stores all over the country."

Released in the ardkore summer of '92, this *Hardcore DJ's...Take Control* compilation landed weeks after Spiral Tribe and other rebel-sound systems turned Castlemorton Common into a week-long autonomous free party zone. Up to 40,000 revellers journeyed to these quaint and sequestered lands in the Malvern Hills to hear "nosebleed" breakbeats from the Tribe and systems like Bedlam, and the "fluffy" house, jazz and soul music from Nottingham renegades DiY, as police helicopters swirled overhead. It looked like hardcore had, indeed, seized control, clogging the nation's motor-arteries with travellers and party-youth eager to get involved.

Most systems managed to evade the police on exiting the site, on May 29, apart from the twelve Tribe members who were arrested, locked up overnight at Worcester police station, and charged the next day with conspiracy to cause a public nuisance. (They would later be trialled as organisers). Their system, trucks and homes were all impounded. When they eventually returned to their North London base, they discovered their homes had been raided by police, personal documents and computers confiscated, and founding member Simone had been arrested. As paranoia turned to anger, Lol Hammond suggested a record deal as a "creative way to fight back," as Mark notes in *A Darker Electricity*. But the capitalist, exploitative music industry was the kind of enemy The Tribe were rebelling against.

The Spirals embodied the tough renegade side of British ardkore, with a hardened sound to match. Within the booming hardcore rave industry, records were much more cheeky and fun. Hazmat-wearing Altern 8 with their groovy bleep for Network Records inverted apocalyptic doom into a laugh, but behind the Vicks-smeared masks and media theatrics, these two were serious Detroit techno musicians; whilst Acen's *Trip To The Moon* triptych for engineering studio Production House elevated sampling to an artform.

British hardcore bypassed traditional pathways to the charts. It was a people's movement, at once pioneering and innovative, "while skirting on the edge of commercial novelty," as rave entrepreneur Richard Russell writes in *Liberation Through Hearing*, with cartoon hits like 'Charly' by The Prodigy (signed by Russell to XL) serving as both igniter – and death sentence for the early purists. "The music was completely alien," adds Jason Warlock. "Sped up breaks, sped up vocals, chopped up bits of other songs. It was a proper carnage of a mosaic, in a beautiful way." He laughs. "Sonically it was a mess because it was made by people literally getting a sampler, chucking stuff in, and having fun with it."

"At the time, ardkore really did seem like some monstrous, amorphous creature, sucking in sound and regurgitating great vomit gusts of anonymous white-label brilliance," writes Simon Reynolds in *Generation Ecstasy*. "Ardkore seethes with a RAGE TO LIVE, to cram all the intensity absent from a week of drudgery into a few hours of fervour," he originally mused from the whitehot crucible of '92 in the first of his continuum-charting essays for *The Wire* magazine. "It's a quest to reach escape velocity. Speed-freak youth are literally running away from their problems, and who can blame them?"

Ardkore was massive, mental, and broadcast on TV via *Top of the Pops*, the *BBC*'s rave program, *Dance Energy*, or *BPM* from *ITV*. But it was also niche, embedded with insider cues, and only for those in the know. Some of the biggest records of the era came with a nod and wink, including Russell's own debut (for Tribal Bass Records) as Kicks Like A Mule with XL partner Nick Halkes, parodying the exclusivity of acid house clubland with the line: "Your name's not down, you're not coming in".

The true ardkore didn't need or heed mainstream media channels, it promoted itself via pirate radio and zines distributed at raves, like *Ravescene*, a black and white A4 photocopy, folded down into A5, set up by Gwen and Josh Lawford and published in from the suburbs of East London. It was a zine for ravers by ravers that ran from 1992 to 1994 producing a total of 51 issues. Carl Cox reviewed records, Claire Henderson wrote about taking drugs safely. With a peak circulation of 40,000 and nationwide distribution, *Ravescene* paved the way for other specialist rave media, like *Eternity*, issued in '92 as a one-colour twenty-pager, which quickly turned into the (self-described) "most controversial underground dance magazine" in the UK, printed in full colour and selling for £1.60 at major newsagents across the country.

Pirate radio was instrumental in distributing the sound, and mobilising the masses, as well as incubating its next generation of DJs. Before becoming the Warlock, one of London's premier underground hardcore and techno DJs, Jason turned his halls of residence in South Woodford into a bedroom radio station. With a self-built circuit board, powered off a car battery, he was broadcasting every Thursday, Friday, Saturday night – "whenever we wanted to put it on," he says. "I was just learning to DJ then on crappy turntables." As ardkore took over the capital, he was spinning three times a week on pirate station Pulse 90.6 FM. But it all came to a sudden end one Tuesday night when the studio door was kicked down by the DTI

(Department of Trade and Industry). "They took all the studio equipment, all my records. I got taken to court and even fined," says Jason. "They might have had a tip-off from some disgruntled DJs who had gotten kicked off the station."

Jason wrote his first tune, 'Warscape', together with Sebastian Vaughan, Spiral Tribe member from the first De-tension parties at Skool House. Seb was just a seventeen-year-old kid from Scotland when he joined the Tribe, busking in London metro stations at weekends to pay for music school in Leeds. "I hadn't found my role yet," he says, "that came later...with Simon."

Simon "Crystal Distortion" Carter, the elder of the two, was already producing and performing when he was "kidnapped" (willingly) by the Tribe. Signed to Rising High records in his teens, as a member of Earth Leakage Trip he minted the first Moving Shadow record, *Psychotronic*, in '91. His records soundtracked many of the founding Spiral raves.

Seb and Simon forged their permanent acid bond rolling down Parliament Hill together one night. There would be bitter fights and fallouts between these two, but also a connection that went deeper than blood, bound up in the cables and constant buzz of their machines, and soaked in LSD punch. They didn't need to speak with words.

"Seb basically came to my squat and was like, get in the van," Simon recalls. "We're going to buy some music equipment, and we want you to choose it all, plug it all in, and show us how to use it. So I got in the van."

"After Castlemorton the police impounded all of the equipment we had," Seb continues. "No more sound system, no more vehicles, nothing. Youth signed a record deal with us, which gave us 40,000 quid."

All the advance money was spent on converting an old trailer into the Spiral Tribe mobile recording studio, which was open to anyone who wanted to collaborate, no matter what level of skill. Spiral Tribe records were collective products, co-creations between any and all Tribe members, engineered by Seb and Simon who would end up performing the music (and writing music from live performances) as the Spiral Tribe Liveset.

Their first Big Life release, *Breach The Peace*, came out in August 1992 with lyrics borrowed from Native American lore reworked into the context of the Tribe's urban rebellion, spliced with news reports over bleepy, percolating acid. Follow-up *Forward The Revolution* landed three months later, sounding like the beginnings of a bad trip. These rebel-rousing singles formed the *Spiral Tribe Sound System* CD album, issued in '93, followed by the double vinyl record, *Tecno Terra,* with a secret message embedded in the cover design that said: "23 Fuck The Law".

On other records they're credited as SP 23, as on their cankerous Rabbit City Records release, *Network 23*, written after a heaving night of raving over a couple of hours between makeshift living room studios – before the mobile studio was fully functional. KISS FM's Colin Faver signed the record to his label after Seb and Simon debuted their improvised survival-techno at Knowledge, London's seminal strictly-techno party happening on Wednesdays at the SW1 Club.

"About a week after we had unboxed the equipment and vaguely got it back together, we had our first gig," Simon recalls. Booked to play with his other music partner, who couldn't make it, Seb willingly jumped in, beginning a musical partnership that has endured, unblinking, on the razor edge of reason for decades. "We did a whole bunch of rubbish," says Simon, "but then two weeks later we were in Rotterdam."

"Once we had our own mobile studio, all things were possible," says Mark. The Spiral convoy and mobile studio rolled through Holland and France, linking up with squatted social centres along the way, including the Blauwe Aanslag in the Hague, where the Acid Planet Bunker punks were twitching in the basement in various comatosed LSD-house states beneath the zap of heavy strobes. Collaborative records like *Out Of The Blue* with Unit Moebius were the first of many co-creations that would turn into the Network 23 label from '94, where records were pressed up and sold out the back of a van, to pay for the petrol to get to the next free party.

"I was often the 'concept guy,'" explains Mark, who had "more extreme tastes" than Seb, who came from acid house, and Simon with his breakbeat hardcore Moving Shadow heritage. Mark was into the Mover, Underground Resistance, and early Bald Terror Rotterdam-style gabber. "With our slightly different angles on the creative process, we meshed perfectly," he continues. "I saw myself as an enabler and a communicator. My work was connecting people, and together we found ourselves at the epicentre of a creative storm."

By the end of '93, the Spiral convoy was parked up in the frozen wastes of Berlin's Potsdamer Platz. A "skeleton crew" would eventually return to the UK for their Crown Court trial, which started on January 10, 1994, leaving the Spiral Tribe Liveset duo to forward the revolution through Europe. Somewhere between a disused factory in Leiden and the Tankhenge of Potsdamer Platz, they came up with the name R-Zac to distinguish themselves from the Tribe, and claim ownership of this new "tekno" music they were making directly from these addled and transient dancefloors.

"The problem we've always had with Spiral Tribe is the fact that it was an open door," Seb explains. "Anyone who wanted to be a part of it, could."

The R-Zac sound was stripped back and pitched up Chicago-jack meets Detroit-groove, rolling and uplifting enough to keep you going through the Tribe's free party endurance-dances. The music was instantaneous and timeless, boisterous and spangled, obliterating all borders between music and self.

"Just keep it on as long as possible. Never switching it off. Never stop," as Simon explained to *DJ Mag*.

After a ten week trial at Wolverhampton Crown Court, the Tribe were finally acquitted for their alleged role in organising Castlemorton, ending nearly two years of legal proceedings at a cost of £4 million. But they could not Kill the Bill that turned them into criminals, and their free party livelihood into a punishable offense.

"They got what they wanted in the end," Seb remarks about the Criminal Justice Bill that was pushed through parliament, as the Tribe stood trial in the Crown Courts. "They changed the laws and made life shit for everyone," says Seb.

"We were gerbils in a cage, experimental mice to these people," remarks Simon.

For the last year of their UK-based operations, the Tribe were under strict and constant police surveillance: "Our phone was tapped, our office was raided several times, we had police helicopters following the sound system around," says Seb, "we either had to stop and disband, or get out of the country." Quitting was not an option.

The Spirals had found the exit and saw that freedom lay ahead, chasing the endless horizon on the open road, and in the constant surge of electricity into sound. These lands will not be silenced, and these machines will never stop. Other tekno-nomads could follow them into the unknown, but they were also free to plot their own route towards whatever future they dared to dream – as long as there was dancing and music, and it was loud.

D.J. WARLOCK

PULSE 90.6FM
TUES- 10pm-12am
SUN- 12am-12pm

TEL: (081)
555 0782.

Artwork: KRIS of RAVESCENE.

RAVESCENE MAGAZEEN

· ROCKIN' THE BOAT 92 · NO 11 ·

WITH A VENGEANCE

SP
23

Hi People, Still Camping + Raving. 5 days of excess at Glastonbury festival. Now the cops have taken the rig + truck etc. I arrived with one record (that I had left in Dannys box in Italy) It took 4 day to borrow Rig geny decks etc but on the last night we got the tekno on.

Live long and Prosper

Keith

Steeped in legend, ancient Glastonbury is believed to be the site of Avalon, the final resting place of King Arthur and Queen Guinevere. Another tradition holds that the Holy Grail, the cup used by Christ at the Last Supper and sought by the Knights of the Round Table, lies buried beneath the Chalice Spring on Glastonbury Tor.

2 - 53 - 04 - 09

SALMON Cameracolour Post Card

Printed in England © J. SALMON LTD., SEVENOAKS, KENT. TEL: (01732) 452381

35

NOTTINGHAM 1.15PM JL 1997

NETWORK 23
19 RUE GEORGES
JOYEUX
95440 ECOUEN
FRANCE

5 012493 020002

VERY FUCKING MENTAL

V F M

VOX 2307

TECHNO

FRANKFURT - ROTTERDAM - NY - LONDON

4

On the corner of Railton Road in Brixton a three-storey Edwardian building stands guard over the frontline. Here street dealers once freely peddled their wares, and cannabis smoke mingled with the heavy reggae music blasting from the shebeens and blues clubs of this West Indian neighbourhood. Since UK Black Panther member Olive Morris squatted a derelict Sunlight laundry in the early '70s, this patch of South London has symbolised autonomous community-building, and outsiders banding together across various social, political and economic divides. It's been home for counter-cultural literature and learning as the 121 Centre from '81, with radical feminists, anarchist squatters, and hardcore techno heads have gathered in the basement for baptisms of extreme electronics in this era of Criminal Injustice.

Launched from the gloom of 1994, Dead By Dawn was one of the many events that took place across all floors of this Brixton heritage site, running for twenty-three strobing editions on the first Saturday of every month. Dead by Dawn was "an open secret, an anonymous pool of power accessible to guileless travellers of multitudinous potentiality," as reviewed in the Spring '95 publication of *Alien Underground* magazine. With its anti-chill-out room on the top floor – the shrill-out lounge – and record stalls and magazines set up on the middle cafe floor, Dead By Dawn put the collective mission of creative and critical reflection into action, as defined by the Praxis label.

Informed by the Situationist, Industrial and Post-Punk (anti-)cultures, and backdropped by failing political systems, Praxis tethered agitating hardcore techno music to discourse, disseminated across newsletters, contextual flyers and correlating *Alien Underground* and *Datacide* zines.

Basel native Christoph Fringeli wrote the first series of Praxis releases through the summer of '92 (as Scaremonger, Metatron and later, Noface) after arriving in South London with some records, a bag of belongings and enough money to survive for a few months.

"His very early techno stuff was the more noisy end of it," reflects Simon Crabb, early Praxis collaborator and electronics member of Bourbonese Qualk, the anarchist art squatters of the Ambulance Station on the Old Kent Road, now living in an entirely occupied row of houses on Malt Street. Simon and Christoph performed the anti-rave techno of *Autonomia* together – the Bourbonese Qualk album signed to Praxis in '93 – with Simon playing live electronics and Christoph DJing; both dressed in the orange splatter camouflage that sleeved the record.

"It was really loud," says Simon, recalling the Dead By Dawn basement where they played in a disorientating fug of smoke and blinding strobes. "Christoph had this obsession with smoke machines and stroboscopes, so basically you couldn't see anything apart from this blinding flashing light right in front of your face. It wasn't at all like a rave, it was very intimidating, very noisy, and confrontational."

Praxis hardcore was the sound of London's counterculture kicking with heavy boots against the mind-numbing status quo. It was techno as "sonic weapon," as described in one of their Newsletters, "but only as long as it doesn't play by the rules, not even its own rules." Every Dead By Dawn began with an exchange of ideas, esoteric and practical, with talks ranging from the *Discourses on Sex Magic and Occulture* by Temple ov Psychick Youth to "what sex would be like in an anarchist society" by the

Lesbian and Gay Freedom Movement. Then everyone would file down treacherous stairs into the basement for hard techno, acid weirdness and a speedcore assault of the senses to bring in the dawn.

The series was catalogued on a double vinyl release (Praxis 23), sold at the final party as a thank you to the community. The compilation included the haunting dark-ambient tribute 'Railton Road Blues' written by Berlin-based Digital Hardcore group Sonic Subjunkies, the schizoid breaks of Welsh brothers Somatic Responses, as well as music from the subnet's American affiliates, including Pittsburgh graffiti artist-turned-rave promoter-DJ (and *Datacide* contributor) Deadly Buda.

"Nothing essential happens in the absence of noise" and "the secret is to hear what you've never heard before" were etched into the final side; its subtitle *The 24th Party* written down the spine. It included audio snippets recorded from Dead By Dawn events, with an inlay of lyrical TechNet texts adding further commentary to London's most radical hardcore meet up in the mid-'90s. The final Dead By Dawn took place on April 6, 1996, serving as a record launch party and farewell to the 121 Centre. The night opened with a discussion about "tearing up plans for the phuture" and closed with a "special blasphemous easter performance" by the masked speedcore satanists, Disciples of Belial, screeching and thrashing in the dark.

"The place was an absolute deathtrap," recalls hardcore record distributor Simon Underground, who had his Underground Music stall set up on the middle floor. Simon, one of the great techno-turntablists of the scene, played records at the third Dead By Dawn, held on April 30, 1994, alongside Spiral Tribe DJ Digit and Jason Warlock, who were all affiliated with Knowledge, London's first weekly meeting spot for this hardlined techno community.

"Knowledge was like walking into some religious experience," says Simon, who first launched his globally renowned vinyl distribution network from a trestle table set up inside the SW1 club, located behind Victoria station. "The club was epic, 300 people on a Wednesday night absolutely going batshit crazy," Simon continues. "You've never seen dancefloors like it."

Underground Music would be the galvanizer of the London hardcore underground, establishing landmark record label links between Paris via Russian Rubik of Mad Dog Distribution, PCP in Frankfurt, and Brooklyn stalwart Lenny Dee. Simon was also the connector between travelling DJs and locals, who would come to his house – or he would go to theirs. Always armed with a box, Simon had as much business savvy as passion. "I knew him before he was even doing parties," says Lenny, "when he started his distribution that's when he started becoming what I call a player, you know, if you have records, you're in the biz. You're a fucking player because it was a game for sure. Try selling some of those records back then. It fucking wasn't easy."

Community building just naturally happened in this nurturing London hardcore underground. "Everybody in the scene wanted everybody else to succeed," says Simon. "Because there was no money in it, there was no backstabbing. Everybody was just into the music and wanted to help push everyone along."

This happened every Wednesday from the sunken pit of the Knowledge dancefloor, ringed with a viewing balcony so you could gaze down and soak it all in. At Knowledge, artists turned up to rave or just hang out, and all the touring techno greats – from Mills to Sven Väth to Paul Elstak – ended up playing their London debuts. "I met Christoph from Praxis there for the first time," reflects Simon, "and got to become friends with Colin Faver. It was a pretty insane time. From sitting at home in mid-'92, listening to Colin on the radio, a year later I was sitting in the studio with him, selling him records."

The two Colins – Dale and Faver – were the main Knowledge residents, both with shows on KISS FM. Faver was the hardcore of the two, pushing things further than Dale would dare. Dale came to techno via Detroit, jazz, soul and funk, DJing at the Hard Club at Gossips from 89 and dancing in clubs with Fabio; Faver was DJing much earlier, as a post-punk in the New Romantic scene playing Tuesday nights in the newly-opened Camden Palace from '82 alongside Eddie Richards. They both joined KISS, separately, when it was a pirate station specialising in rare groove.

Dale's Abstract Dance show featured artist interviews and purist Detroit-style techno, running until 1999. Colin Faver's more cutting-edge broadcasts happened every Tuesday night, right before Knowledge, and early Sunday evenings, premiering unsigned London techno talent on a segment called "demo DAT pressure". Aphex Twin, Spiral Tribe and Force Mass Motion were all signed to Faver's Rabbit City Records label from demos sent to KISS; whilst Aphex and Spiral DJs like Digit and Kim Cosmik were regularly booked for Knowledge (just like the Tresor club and label dynamic in Berlin).

"I don't think we expected anything from it, really," says Dale. "It was a Wednesday night playing techno" – before techno had broken in the UK – "but we had a six o'clock licence and London was really hungry for that sound. It was really fresh, not many people were doing it, and the club just exploded."

Initiated by rave promoter Jane Howard as a place for breakbeat DJs on her rolodex to play their Eurotechno records, the guestlist from opening night, on February 12, included people like Kevin Mullins, promoter of Rage at Heaven, with whom Jane started working in the '70s promoting punk bands, before moving into legal raves like Raindance and the members-only club Interdance at Sterns in sleepy Worthing.

Jane was the real driving force, admits Dale: "Jane suggested we do a club, she was like, 'leave it all to me'." She had some wild ideas – and Dale admits they didn't always see eye to eye. "She had that free party mentality," he says, "there were times we didn't connect, and I'm probably as stubborn as she was, so we used to fight quite a lot. We had a full-blown fight about the direction the club was going in, and I ended up leaving."

When Dale left, he was replaced by Loftgroover, then playing "heavy techno house" with partner Ron Wells as Techno Bros – "a mickey-take on Bros, the pop band. Nothing we ever did was serious, it was jokes all day," says Wells – and dark outlier techno as one of the most devastatingly solid DJs on the early London rave scene. "It was almost like he was using the sync button with turntables," continues Wells. "He was absolutely solid. His sets felt like being hit with a sledgehammer."

Loft would become one of the hardest of the British hardcore techno contingent, thanks to some "gentle ribbing" from Simon, but that would come later. "I got chatting to him because he always used to play the bloody pinball machine next to my record store," says Simon. "He'd be constantly asking me for 50 pence pieces, knowing I had a nice float. I said, maybe if you buy some records, I'll give you change in 50 pence pieces." He laughs, "we always had good banter and got to be friends."

"We didn't say it's going to be a really hard techno club when we started," says Dale, "although after a while it went that way. Techno was getting to the point where people didn't mind what it was as long as it was fast and hard. And that's when I left, because I still loved the techno – just not at 160 BPM."

Way out in the sticks, in a Wandsworth warehouse south of the Thames, one of the biggest editions of the Brixton hardcore basement party, VFM, is grinding across two areas: doomsday techno from Frankfurt and Praxis sonic-hostility whips up the Knowledge crowd, who now have to get their techno fix over a weekend, like normal people. And in the second room a long-haired nerd is banging out caustic *Analogue Bubblebath* bangers and euphoric ambient music. This is Very Fucking Mental indeed. It's May 14, 1994, and the hardcore resistance is mounting against the Criminal Justice

Bill – fighting the raving injustice with raves!

Inspired by the "magic" of the pre-CJB scene, and incensed by the "fucking police" crackdowns and the raids that followed, VFM brought illegal rave culture to the mid-'90s London club scene. Launched from beneath the streets of Brighton Terrace in early '93, VFM would grow out of its humble basement beginnings over the next few years, but also further away from the crew's original vision, which is why it ended sooner than it should.

VFM siphoned a singular mix of menacing isolation tank techno brewing across London and Frankfurt. It was affordable – £6 entry before 3 AM, £3 after – had no dress code – just "dress to sweat" – and went on 'til late. "We aligned ourselves very much with Spiral Tribe and that anarchic aspect," explains co-founder Jason Mendonca, the metal guitarist behind some of the Praxis label's most "abjectly horrible and unpleasant" satanic speedcore as Disciples of Belial.

Together with his two housemates, Jason launched VFM as a party for people to "go mental to really loud nasty music", supplied by local residents from the hardcore squat party scene and the banging midweek basement clubs Jason and crew were frequenting at the time, like Eurobeat 2000, where he first encountered the Praxis chief playing with Simon Crabb in the posh basement Tea Room of the Regent Palace Hotel near Piccadilly Circus.

An "uncool kid" from suburban London, into heavy metal and the occult from an early age, evil humour masks the genuine pain and rage that seethes through Jason's range of electronic projects, from the cult Praxis-signed Disciples of Belial – "dashed off in fifteen minutes, because it made me laugh," admits Jason – to the ingenious Lorenz Attractor studio collaboration with Jason Warlock. There's also Neuroviolence, which launched his crew's record label, Zero Tolerance, with more PCP-nuance and dark breakbeats amidst the rinsing speedcore, as VFM was coming to a painful end.

Jason was deeply traumatised from childhood, which he processed through music and being completely wild on stage. "Most of my earlier pre-therapy musical endeavours were spawned by nihilism, hatred and self-loathing," he says. "The guy who gave those performances in whatever guises was genuinely angry. So if I could get up on stage and play the most atonal aggressive music and scream my head off like a banshee, I could let all this anger out, without actually hurting anyone – other than myself."

Christoph became a resident at VFM, and Jason played at Dead By Dawn; musically there were crossovers, but ideologically these were polar parties, as Jason explains: "Those guys already had intellectual ideas about Marxism and the struggle of the urban proletariat and whatnot, and we were just fucking maniacs."

Both were driven by social activism, VFM just took a more "direct action" approach by raising money for the homeless, choosing to circumvent the "nefariousness" of charities by doing the charity work themselves: "With the money from the early VFM parties we bought blankets off this bloke Joe Bananas" – Ian "Lenny" Leonard, founder of the infamous Joe Bananas Blanket Stall at Glastonbury, next to the Pyramid Stage – "Spiral Tribe lent us a van, because we didn't have any wheels, and Ian Blatchford, who ran the phone line with Debbie, drove us around the Bull Ring down in SE1, distributing the blankets."

VFM has various meanings. "It stood for whatever you wanted to," says Jason, "Very Friendly Movement. Very Fucking Mental. Value For Money..." Whilst its music policy remained fairly consistent over its three years as it evolved into the larger all-nighters in Stratford, and finally taking over two rooms – The Bunker and The Laboratory – at Club Essence in Bromley by Bow in East London.

The end of VFM was a dark time for Jason, marred by constant police presence. "They started turning up to our events and searching everybody before they went in, and camping in the car park outside," says Jason:

the new CJB in effect, or possibly sabotage from inside the community. "There were some very underhanded goings-on in the scene at that time," he says. "Then things got really really dark and it just became more and more unpalatable until it petered out."

VFM's demise chimed with a sweeping gentrification of London, where favourite community boozers were shutting down and getting replaced by soulless chain pubs, public drinking was banned, and council properties were sold off to the highest bidder. It was also becoming notoriously difficult to squat in an ever more surveilled and controlled city. Christoph from Praxis spent the end of the '90s sleeping between sofas and office tables, after he was violently evicted from his squat (with firebombs). Even the 121 Anarchist Centre on Railton Road was eventually shut down in August 1999, ending twenty-six years of occupation – and a seven-month siege, triggered when the 121 squatters lost possession of the building that was legally theirs to claim. "There are always 'technicalities,'" reported *Datacide* at the time, "part of a cynical cleaning up process by Lambeth Council that is trying to attract "wealth" to the area."

Ever resourceful, the 121 squatters launched several publicity campaigns to raise awareness of their fight against the bulldozer and the gavel, including an "invasion" of Lambeth Town Hall and a Drink-In (against the new anti-Street-Drinking by-law). On April 10 the squatters massed 500 people on the surrounding streets to celebrate 86 days of resistance, to dance (some stripped naked) to hip hop and the Clash from sound systems and drink beers together in one last act of rebellion.

Even with the new stop and search police powers, the hardcore techno resistance kept resisting. "Only free parties can save free parties!!!" was the mission of the international sound system coalition United Systems, formed shortly after the first CJA arrests and system seizures in the Spring of '95, kicking off the next noisy phase of London's warehouse scene, occupied by the next generation of rebel-sound systems that proliferated in the capital.

"It became harder to put on legal parties and book people because, what was the incentive to pay when you could go out for nothing?" says Simon Underground, who launched his clubnight, Live Evil, on the final freezing Thursday of January '97. The first event took place at the Powerhouse in Finsbury Park; another London countercultural landmark caught in the undertow of capitalism, where politicised youth of the '70s and '80s danced and fought and drank beer together when it was known as the Sir George Robey pub, before the Mean Fiddler Music Group took over in 1996.

The second Live Evil returned to Brixton that June, to Club 414, with another hardcore PA battle between its Australian obnoxious cheapcore brothers, Bloody Fist, pirate radio DJ Traffik from Energy FM, and Simon's own Suicide Squad featuring Max Death playing on outmoded Macintosh gear. The party was in collaboration with infamous speedcore night Rampant, later damned in the music presses as "the most diabolical club in Britain" by Jacques Peretti in *The Face* in September 1997; and the slanderous *Nazi Gabber Hell* tabloid piece by Lee Harpin for the *Daily Star* one month later (which ended in a court case).

"You might stop the party but you can't stop the future," rapped the Spirals at the start of the era; who had since dissolved into splinter sound system tribes, forced to party in exile, as Live Evil was coming to the fore. Safely rooted within the dirty yellow brick walls of the Electrowerkz in Islington from 2001, undeterred by media or musical trends, Live Evil flourished into London's longest-running hardcore techno night, playing the evil music that its community lived for.

bring yourselves, your friends, food and drink, drums, instruments, paint, brushes, chalk, banners, things for workshops, info stalls, weird shit, etc..

MARK.N BLOODY FIST, AUSTRALIA
MANU LE MALIN BLOC 46, FRANCE
HELLFISH DEATHCHANT
SIMON UNDERGROUND UM
DEATHMACHINE DEVIL'S BROOD, CORRUPT
MATT GREEN CORRUPT, EPILEPTIK
DARKSIDE CORRUPT
MAX DEATH TUFF SHIT
DCS FCK RECORDS, DENMARK
FOR DJ AND LIVE PA TIMES AND INFO CHECK OUT
UM RECORD STALL
22.00-06.00 ENTRANCE £5 B4 23.00 (& cons.) £8 AFTER
NOVEMBER 12TH 2004
@ ELECTROWERKZ
7 Torrens Street London EC1V 1NQ

FUCKING HOSTILE

5

Nobody turned more people hardcore than Lenny Dee. Short in stature, big, bold and loud in everything else, when people first encountered this firecracker from Sheepshead Bay in Brooklyn, they were infected by his vision. "I felt that I was part of this revolution," he says animatedly, "and bringing hard music to the forefront was my fucking goal." With exuberance and passion in abundance, everything he did, he did to the extreme. "I'm a hardcore person," he declares, "meaning that I express my shit out into music."

By the time of his own awakening to hardcore – that explosive Mayday Cologne set in the spring of '92 – Lenny was an experienced DJ and producer, one of the most celebrated on the bill. In New York he had engineered gold records from some of the most legendary studios in Manhattan, and was collaborating with British heroes like New Order and the KLF. Orbital Rave stars Carl Cox and Caspar Pound from cult label Rising High Records were amongst his closest friends and confidants. Since issuing his first records in the mid-'80s – several of them soundtracking the '88 British Second Summer of Love – Lenny had cycled through high BPM roller disco music, New York freestyle and bedroom breakbeats with his partner Frankie Bones; and now he was crashing down on the continent, getting into the harder and heavier side of the Eurotechno emerging from Germany, Belgium and the Netherlands.

After nearly a decade in music, he'd hit a critical moment. "I was at the pivoting point," Lenny explains, should he follow the techno route to keep his career going, or should he continue down this harder, less travelled path? "I found that I reached the end, and that's what hardcore was to me," he says. "When everyone was saying: 'why don't you get out of this?' I said: no!" Lenny leaned in – and took the rest of Brooklyn's diehard outlaws with him.

Growing up in the cultural melting pot of Brooklyn's southernmost district, where the city's wide boulevards gave way to beaches and funfairs, music was everywhere, and an obsession from an early age. Disco and Hi-NRG soundtracked the parent-free weekends and balmy summers of these outer borough youths. The movie *Beat Street* and its Arthur Baker score, meanwhile, had turned the nation on to breakbeats and b-boy culture. Ferried outwards from the ruin of the Bronx, together with graffiti – the literal art of making your mark, hip hop taught the kids of the street to dream, and dream big. Fighting and petty crime were the alternative; and the blood ran hot in this immigrant 'hood.

"This was a place and a time where a burner and a bulletproof vest were regarded as essential fashion accessories," as investigative journalist Frank Owen posed in *Clubland*; crime literally bled into the pavement.

First paired up with the younger Frankie Bones, these Original Gangsters of Freestyle were passionate, driven – and competitors from the start. "We used to be enemies," says Lenny. "Brooklyn was like this big creative camaraderie of different people that really really brought electronic music to New York." He adds: "Everybody had their own goals but the main thing was the music." Others, including Omar Santana and Joey Beltrum (both from Queens) joined the Brooklyn cohort to bring electronic music to the outer boroughs, via student radio and youth club nights.

Whilst his friends were buying pot, Lenny was buying records. Holed up in his bedroom, away from the "trouble" outside, he honed his craft, playing Run DMC, Kat Mandu and Kraftwerk "like a lunatic" on turntables he earned from cleaning his uncle's store. Music would be his escape from this dead end backwater, an hour's train ride from Manhattan, where pop stars were made and DJs like Jellybean Benitez were worshipped as gods; and Lenny wanted in.

Determined to prove himself, and to his parents, that he could make a career out of music, that he was going to be a success, he enrolled on a production course at the Institute of Audio Research. It wasn't long before one of the most renowned studios offered him the job of a lifetime – which he accepted, working for Arthur Baker at Shakedown, and engineering multiple hit records with pop stars (remixing New Order's 'Confusion' was his first big project.)

"I was a pig in shit," Lenny exclaims. "But I was going to school at the same time. That was insanity." He describes recording at Shakedown all through the night, passing out on the office couch and waking up to go to school, only to head straight back to Shakedown after classes for another all-nighter. "Obviously I fucked up at school," Lenny continues. "My parents never saw me. And the DJing was kicking off as well."

From 1990 Lenny was "a constant jetlagged mess" living between his home in New York and the couches and tour buses of an endless techno-tour to bring hardcore to the fucking world, and turn the world fucking hardcore! It was mentally, physically and emotionally exhausting. "I didn't even know what country I was in. I got so fucked up with that, I had to go to the doctor," he says. "I couldn't tell you the day, the time, the month, the year. The doctor was like, you fly more than pilots."

But it was worth it. "Even though I was sleeping on the floor and we were all fucking broke as broke can be," he says, "all my friends were stuck on the corner getting into trouble, and I was the one that got out."

Lenny's constant touring, and ear for talent, enabled him to create the first international hardcore network. But as a trained studio engineer, preferring to write music in collaboration, Industrial Strength didn't become a channel for his own music. "My label was never about me," he says. "Some records are kind of weird and odd, and you think 'Why did I release that,' but at the time a lot of these guys needed support, and I wasn't so critical." Lenny curated people, not records; acting as a galvaniser and mentor for the younger talents he banded together into a motley crew, an outlaw family.

Industrial Strength techno hardened into hardcore as soon as that first PCP sampler ripped through Cologne ice stadium. "Hard music and hardcore, it's really about what pisses you off," he says. "How do you release that tension? And provoke a reaction." The answer ripped through Manhattan during the blood boiling summer of 1994.

"Double pack of banging assault that is just h.a.r.d.a.s.f.u.c.k." ran *Alien Underground*'s review of *Industrial Power '9d4,* the debut album from Disciples Of Annihilation (DOA), a ten track sucker punch of gangster movie samples, distortion and catchy hardcore songwriting – and "a worthwhile introduction to the new genre of swear word traxx," stated the underground zine. "This has the dark energy of people who take no shit."

Lenny was "blown away" when he heard DOA's raw and powerful demo, with tracks like 'Ya Mutha' featuring an abusive phone recording sampled over a brutal bludgeoning of Rotterdam-inspired gabber kick drums, and the slower psychedelic death-trip of 'Poisoned With Strychnine' – one of Sal's mental and mental-inducing solo productions. "The DOA sound was like its own language," says fellow member Carl Carinci, the established producer of the group as a member of United Rave States, who tributed the Netherlands in their Belgium-signed 12" debut, *Sunrise In Rotterdam.*

Carl was turned on to production by Joey Beltram in early 1990, seeing the Mentasm master writing from his Brooklyn studio. "It was there I learned about the MPC drum machine," he recalls. "I went out and purchased one and from that point all I thought about was making music." He insists Sal is the real engineer "who brought insanity to life," says Carl. "I could tell right away he had a vision. Sal said he wanted to make tracks in the 220 to 250 BPM range. At the time nothing like that existed."

"I was more into guitar and playing in bands," adds Sal. "Guitar was my first instrument, the hardcore techno stuff came many years later."

Sal wasn't a DJ, unlike Carl and Nicky Marchetti, who'd met through the 1990 Queens rave scene. Nicky "Fingers" Marchetti was the third member and real DJ talent of the crew, who had one of NYC's first techno mix shows with Carl on WCWP, a campus radio station from Long Island University. DOA came together at the Numbers Records store in Queens, where Nicky worked. "They played me the United Rave States record and I said to myself: 'I need to up my game here,'" continues Sal. "I tried to meld the energy of thrashy guitar music with the hardcore techno at the time. I guess you could call me 'The Walter White of hardcore techno.'"

Nicky was the catalyst and "visionary" of the group. He was also the "party guy," say Carl and Sal, who (unlike Nicky) never attended the Storm Raves that Frankie Bones with his Groove Records crew brought to Brooklyn and Staten Island between 1991 and '92. "We held our own illegal raves around NYC," they say, which were "raw with zero commercial influences."

DOA made their rebellious NYC debut together with Temper Tantrum in July '94, promoting their debut record – and Industrial Strength's new take no prisoners guitar-punk sound – as more than 8,000 people from all over the world descended on the capital for the penultimate edition of the New Music Seminar. Here at the Sheraton Hotel, deals were brokered and careers made – at the expense of the recording artists and performers, who had to buy their way into it. With registration fees between $380 and $440, and various other promotional costs, including $20 just to submit a tape to the booking committee, the New Music Seminar was "a veritable gold mine," reported the New York Times; and a bit of a scam. It was the perfect platform for Industrial Strength to tear up the system.

"Sal definitely said some dumb shit on the mic, which might have offended some folks...ahhh fuck em. Their scene sucked. We were here to take over," they laugh.

Heavy-metal hardcore would define Industrial Strength through the mid-'90s, with guitars first appearing on the label's 10th release, *The Trauma EP*, by Baltimore duo Glitch. It's 'Heavy Mental' B-side showcased unbridled riffs locking horns with the thunderous bang of the 909 in a funky skirmish between the moshpit and the dancefloor, a space Industrial Strength would claim under the banner of *New York City Speedcore*, coined by DOA with DJ Narcotic in their track together. Speedcore would later become a denotation of tempo, but DOA weren't bound by BPMs: "We just went with what we were feeling at the time," says Sal. "If it was fast, great. Shit, I had a slower, trancy release right after that. So, anything goes in terms of BPMs. Put a label on it, whatever. It's all good."

There was also the DJ Skinhead name, used as an ambiguous umbrella moniker for Industrial Strength's thrashcore to unleash their most brutal and barbarous productions. It was inaugurated by a reworking of some Texan metal legends into one of the most iconic pieces of American Fucking Hostile techno. Then came 'Extreme Terror', whetted into an anti-war tool in the era of the War on Terror. But it started out as a bit of a laugh between lads during the lull hours between shows on tour through the UK.

"We were sitting in Carl [Cox]'s house listening to some fucking Industrial Strength tracks and then Darrien [Kelly] goes: Extreeeeeeeme Terrrrrrrror! We were saying that for weeks, every single day," says Lenny. "We even had Carl [Cox] doing it, because we were just so fucking into it. When I came back I had the guys do 'Extreme Terror'. I said, This is the hook, we don't need anything else, just fucking do it."

Under Mayor Rudi Giuliani's own reign of terror, DJ Skinhead was the sound of the outer boroughs outlaws partying against the sweeping gentrification and "dance police" raids that crippled NYC's rave scene over the second half of the '90s. Sworn in at the start of '94, one of the most ruthless District Attorneys of the '80s would become the scourge of the New York City night community after turning his fight against the mob into a war on drugs and the nightclubs he saw as fuelling demand. Through aggressive and wholesale enforcement of the Cabaret Law, created in 1926 to repress NYC's mutli-ethnic clubs during Prohibition by banning dancing in venues without a cabaret licence, the man who "cleaned up New York" also bulldozed one of the greatest clubbing capitals of the world.

"Put 25,000 people in an aircraft hangar in Brooklyn and you're going to walk away with casualties," Frankie Bones commented to *Rave* magazine in 1990 whilst touring the UK as Flowmasters with Tommy Musto. If he wanted to bring this radical youth movement back home to the outer boroughs, he had to start small, and build a dedicated following first.

Frankie began his DIY career slinging mixtapes from a car stereo shop inside Caesar's Bay Bazaar, a giant flea market-style shopping centre on the waterfront of Sheepshead Bay, and DJing at local teen nights. Like the Pied Piper of Brooklyn, he mobilised his acolytes from the Groove Records store, opened on Avenue U on April 21, 1990.

"The first Groove Records on Avenue U was the best thing that could have happened to South Brooklyn," says Maria 909, who grew up on Lenny and Frankie's mixtapes before becoming a promoter herself. "Every single record in that shop was an instant classic. I used to rollerblade from Coney Island all the time and it was my favourite place to go during the day."

Groove's policy was strictly anti-commercial, "just the music that opens your mind," as described by Frankie's brother, Adam X, speaking to *Frontpage* in November 1992. Adam worked the counter, with Damon Wild running the mail order. Heather Heart completed the team, whose rave zine *Under One Sky* with its Sonic Groove Records reviews was influential in shaping satellite hardcore scenes across the US. Groove Records wasn't about making money; "we use the shop more like the base of operations," adds Adam.

From Groove they planned the word of mouth parties that would eventually turn into Storm, which started with just 200 people coming together in a brickyard in Flatbush on May 11, 1991. One year later the crew were booking international stars like Sven Väth, Richie Hawtin and Caspar Pound to play in a dodgy warehouse, flight cases precariously balanced on crates serving as the DJ booth. This was the Brain Storm edition on June 20, held over the New Music Seminar weekend – as UR debuted at the Limelight.

"In 1989, Frankie Bones became the only American DJ to become part of the London Orbital Rave Scene," proclaimed the flyer. "In 1990 Storm was his vision, in 1991 that vision became a reality. In 1992, with the help of the Storm organisation and the 2,500 people at our last rave, Storm became a legacy... Come and Join the Future."

With a $15 entrance fee, this was not a free party rave, just an unlicensed one: New York's Official Hardcore Rave. The Storm crew moved into a licensed venue that October – "100% legal, 100% underground, 100% pure" – launching the "first and only true Euro-style techno club" in the outer boroughs. This was the Thunderground, housed in an ancient converted wine cellar in Staten Island, with psychedelic meltdown rooms, mind-dissolving lasers and "the most pounding techno sound ever in NYC". Frankie Bones, Adam X and Jimmy Crash played opening night in the Techno Reactor with Ralphie Dee in the Nuclear Chamber.

Two months after the opening of Thunderground, in the midst of a blizzard that blanketed the entire East Coast in snow, the crew threw their last illegal rave in an icy Staten Island horse barn. "In the beginning, we stood alone. A small gathering of friends in celebration of the dance. This dance became known as Rave and we are no longer alone," stated the flyer. But the scene had gotten too big for the Groove records purists. They were ready to bow out and head back underground. "It seems that now everyone wants to throw R+++S, dress like R+++RS and so on..." Frankie opined in the corresponding December issue of *Under One Sky*, "At this point it's not hard to play 'hardcore,' or to make a 'hardcore' record. It is hard to live a 'hardcore' life."

Storm signalled the birth of rave in NYC, but they were not strictly hardcore events. From the end of Storm, the real hardcore outlaw era emerged with crews like Digital Domain, Satellite Records and Uptown Underground seizing the bridges, burnt out warehouses and ballparks of the outer boroughs for a year of endless partying. Industrial Strength techno was the sound these ravers were clamouring to hear.

"I've been waiting for this for seven years," Lenny exclaimed after playing Brooklyn ruffneck hits like Ralphie Dee's 'Totally Cained' to kids in ISR shirts and face masks, crowding round the DJ booth to watch the chief's fingers fly across these waxy munitions for the second edition of Satellite Production's epic Voyager Raves, based inside the Brooklyn Bridge anchorage. It was April 1995, and the hardcore outlaws were taking over.

"To finally come here again, and play techno music – whereas before I was outcast; it was worth the wait." Lenny had just turned twenty-seven, and was still hesitant about the future of techno in America, especially in New York. But that night, amongst 3,000 Bridge and Tunnel Youths losing it to Industrial Strength techno crammed inside the cement bowls of Brooklyn's most iconic landmark, the future could go to hell because that was one mutha of a trip.

FIGHTING SPIRIT

6

In the City of Light and Love, a teenage runaway with a dark past searches for family amongst the street gangs of Courbevoie. He's a lone wolf, hackles raised and ready for danger – welcoming it, even. This one was wild, antisocial, and a lover of music from the womb. The wolf becomes his insignia, but he's more of a werewolf: a musical shapeshifter dressed always in black and, on the surface, as intimidating as the music he plays. But this is just a mask, one of the many he wears against the harsh glare of the public; disguises that have simultaneously freed and imprisoned him over the years.

"Without the music, my life would have been between four walls or planks of wood in the ground," says Emmanuel "Manu" Dauchez, "because my life was not funny at all." Before becoming "Le Malin", the evil one, Manu was deep into Ska, Punk, Soul, and Trojan Records. But every concert attended ended in a fight, more often with him on the ground, "which was cool."

Then Manu discovered rave, sometime in 1991, and at last felt peace. "The only thing I remember is the day after," reflects the "Black Duck" of the French Touch, and the burning soul of Parisian hardcore. "I went back to my hotel room where I was living with my girlfriend and said: 'I found something. Something is happening...' I was on LSD and drawing a circle and trying to explain that I was in the middle of the circle trying to get out. I had a good time, but at the same time I was like, I'm locked."

From the age of ten, Manu was living alone in a hotel room. "My friends were monsters, fear, horror. Violence, too, was fascinating to me," he says in the documentary *Sous Le Donjon*, about Astropolis, his adopted rave family and France's longest-running festival, where he's been a resident since 1997.

Manu learnt to DJ as "a way for me to talk, to express myself, to open myself to others," he says. "When you don't trust yourself any more and you don't trust people, music brings you closer together than you think." When Manu discovered rave he went "all in," as his friend and former manager Antoine Caudron (AKA DJ Kraft) puts it in *Sous Le Donjon*. "He's always been so sincere in everything he's done, that eventually he got consumed by it," adds Manu's other friend, mentor and champion, Laurent Garnier. "When he's playing he's a master, a slave driver" – or The Driver, for techno sets – says Garnier in *Sous Le Donjon*. "Manu is an urban warrior, a diamond in the rough."

"There were all these rivalries brewing all the time. It often got out of hand," Garnier says, recalling being treated as a "pariah"; barred from the early raves in Paris, because he played in clubs, and damned by the hardcore scene as a techno artist for playing "commercial pap."

"If you're hardcore, you're hardcore, and that's it," says Manu, unwilling to linger on the painful schisms that made him seek musical alliances elsewhere. "You didn't go to clubs and listen to Garnier, as I did," Manu continues. "But I said, 'I'm going to do whatever I want to do, go wherever I want to go, and play whatever I want to play. I was playing techno, hardcore, playing at a club, a free party, no boxes, no labels."

Parisian discotheques of the French Touch era were chic, champagne bottle service, for jet-setters. Rave was relegated to the warehouse, and even then, there was resistance from the French authorities. From July '93, when Oz (organised by Laurent Garnier with Coda magazine) was cancelled the day before 18,000 people were set to descend upon the Parc des Expositions in Amiens, techno was demonised in the French media and heavily policed by local authorities, with increasing brutality. Infrastructure for hardcore raves and club nights became scarce, and were fiercely defended by the city's burgeoning DJs and promoters.

"Places were expensive, and the crews who had access to them were very defensive," says Parisian journalist and speedcore promoter, Florian Pittion-Rossillon. Competition was fierce between territorial and seriously invested artists, who would rather "kill each other," as he puts it, than collaborate: "I don't have any factual information implicating this or that person. I just have a prism of analysis," he adds as a caveat. "Everything quickly turned into permanent wars."

"The scene was really active. We all knew each other, and we don't know each other: Parisian politics," says Manu. "The hardcore was really serious, though. No cheese at all. That's a French thing: we eat the cheese, we don't play it."

Manu learnt to mix on a set of cheap turntables (one without pitch control) and started obsessively collecting records to play over and over again whilst still in the "psychedelic vibe" of the rave. "I went deep into the core," he says, "and I don't mean hardcore." He spent the first half of the '90s going from rave to rave to club to afterparty, only returning home to mix until the next one. He didn't know how to break his way in, so in the beginning he turned up to raves with record bags, hoping for a set: "I wanted to be part of it so hard that, yeah, it blocked me in a way because I was too intense," he admits. "We don't talk about booking fee or anything. I just wanted to play." Every Sunday he was under the Pont de Tolbiac Bridge to experience Jérôme Pacman play trippy after hours trance back to back with DJ Armand and DJ Sonic. "I really liked the way they played: mixing the records to the very end of the track, all together, all the time," he says.

Manu would turn this seamless and excursive style into his own slow burning form of hardcore, creating a "symphonica of noise," as Jeff Mills once described it, and DJing with the kind of flamboyant irreverence of someone who knows his collection by touch. It soon got him noticed by Mills' agent Frédéric Djaaleb, who – alongside Garnier and Lenny Dee – were the first to give Manu a chance.

His first major DJ gig happened on November 7, 1992, opening and closing Tribal No Limit at Le Bourget Exhibition Center in front of 6,000 people. From the mid-'90s Manu was touring most weekends through Europe, technically on par with (and billed alongside) early rave's great turntablists like Jeff Mills and Liza N Eliza, the Queen of Psychedelia.

Just like Tanith in Berlin, Manu was a raver. On Sundays in Paris, still awake from the weekend, he would head straight from the gig to a free party in a warehouse, or drive two hours to some field outside of Paris, to play, or just to be continually immersed in the rave. "Every weekend we did crazy stupid things," he reflects, "I organised some party in the basement of a club, without the owner even knowing!"

There was also the "official" Sunday afterparty he hosted with Liza N Eliaz, sneaking 500 people to party for twelve hours in the dusty concrete warren beneath the Montparnasse train station, one of the busiest transport links in Paris. Somehow they managed to set up a sound system, directly beneath the police station. Officers eventually turned up because the station was shaking from the bass. "I made a flyer, really discreet, act low," says Manu, "Don't do any foolish things on the street because otherwise they're gonna stop us. I think Paris is the only city where you can do it. Nowadays you can't do this anymore."

Liza was a huge influence on Manu, responsible for that first life-saving rave experience: "I always say Liza N Eliaz because it's the first souvenir I have," he says.

Liza was luminous in the dark, harsh Parisian warehouse rave scene, playing her fun and intoxicating style of speedcore alongside Laurent Hô at Tekno Tanz in May '92, and a popular resident for Patrick Rognant's landmark *Rave Up* shows on Radio FG. Wearing a psychedelic look to match her colourful cartoonish sets, which packed depth and nuance over three or four turntables and layers of tape edits, she was often dressed in hand painted outfits made by her artist partner Yvette Neliaz (where her name comes from).

Liza was a true hardcore musician, deeply invested in her craft, always performing with head down, eyes locked into the mix. "For me, DJing is actually more live than a so-called live act," she explained to *Raveline* in 1996. "The constant search for hidden exits by adding something to certain sequences and subtracting it from the previous one, cutting it off and letting it flow back again, is actually the same as playing a conventional instrument."

Originally from Ostend on the Belgium coast, and assigned male at birth, Liza was playing keyboards (as Liza Lotta) in various new wave rock groups, and supporting Neon Judgement in 1987 before joining the rave scene. She preferred making cut-ups with tape than simplistic Roland machines. "I wasn't exactly thrilled with the TB 303," she admitted to *Raveline*, with acid house and EBM nearly passing her by. "A lot of people thought at the time, including me, that the bassline was a silly thing that you could maybe use on the train to sketch out melodies, but other than that: rubbish. Oh well."

Liza turned into a figurehead for experimental acid, collaborating with Amsterdam pioneer Dano on speedy funcore for Mokum, like 'Energy Boost' and a heavy-mental remix of Fear Factory issued on the Dutch gabber label's *F**king Hardcore* compilation series in '96. Moving (briefly) to Amsterdam in '89 and hearing Eddy Leclerc at the RoXY was the "flash" that turned Liza away from keyboards and into her hardcore vinyl head trips, delivered at high velocity. In Holland she was christened the Queen of Terror, which never suited Liza or her music, as partner Yvette explained to *Tsugi*: "She couldn't stand the nickname," she says. "She didn't intend to terrorise people. She saw her music as something joyful and not at all mean, dark. It even had a very cartoonish side."

Liza's music was powerful and empowering, working on multilayers, appealing to the seriousness and severity of the sparring Frenchcore scene, and the more party-driven gabbers of Holland where she was equally deified. Tracks like 'I Don't Wanna Say' featuring lyrics from The Exciters, 'He's Got the Power' – "He makes me do things I don't wanna do / He makes me say things I don't wanna say" – were pitched up to seem like another kiddie hardcore tune, albeit a creepy one. Nestled in swollen didgeridoo bass and Curly-style esoterica, with a shuddering barrage of kickdrums to keep you screwfaced through the trip, the track became a free party classic when it was posthumously released by friend and collaborator Laurent Hô.

Liza mostly released through USA Import Records in Antwerp, making her international debut with Industrial Strength together with Manu on the 1995 sampler that launched the Brooklyn label's five year alliance with British grindcore label Earche. Liza and Manu served up polar promo mixes, selecting very different music from the ISR catalogue, which included the happier gabber sublabel, Ruff Beats, and the purer techno-driven IST Records. These diverse mixes are testament not only to Manu and Liza's individual styles, but the wide range of hardcore Lenny was curating through the decade.

Noisy, bubbly and bounding, with feminised vocal hooks and bright shades of discordant noise, Liza's *Romper Stomper* mix is as joyous as it is slamming, packing in lots of happier hits like Lenny Dee & Dark Raver's 'Toda Rhythm' and the scurrilous 'Make My Day' by Cocoricco resident DJ Cirillo. Always supportive of her female peers, Liza includes 'Force Factor' from Detroit hard techno trailblazer Laura Grabb (a former rap records engineer turned hardwired hardware artist with her Cipher label, active until '99).

Manu flaunts his ingenuity via the yin-yang musical pairings and clever sequencing of his own *Paris Hardcore DJ Mix*, which happens right at the start with the oppressive and riffy 'Heavy Mental' from Baltimore duo Glitch sandwiching ISR's earliest and most pop-friendly release, 'Start The Panic'. Later he pitches down records, elevating the artful rhythmic noise of a track like 'Follow The Leader' (Lenny's collaboration with Ralphie Dee as English Muffin) into the gurgling acid of John Selway and Oliver Chelster's nightmare trance 'In The Sun' as Disintegrator (ISR's first homegrown techno signing). Compared to Liza's, Manu's mix is a more progressive, techno-informed slipstream listen, which teases you seductively into the Fuckin Hostile-Extreme Terror maelstrom of 200 BPM guitar-core that closes. This was the sound of Manu stepping outside of his comfort zone, but still owning it.

Setting the pace well below the norm, Manu's borderless and burning musical vision made him equally revered and feared in the French scene. He turned painful personal experiences into powerful and empowering DJ sets, and the Parisian scene politics into armour. "That culture was so important to me, every time I felt or I saw something that's not right, I had to fight for it – or against it," he says.

"They didn't realise that the more they were trying to block me, the more I was ready to burn them all, with turntables. They gave me the strength and the fire to be Manu Le Malin, the fucking needle in your shoes."

"I don't want people to be happy when I am playing my tunes. I WANT THEM TO FEEL VIOLENCE!" When Londoner Loftgroover said this to *Eternity* in 1995, happy hardcore escapism was taking over nut nut Britain – so he was starting moshpits in the rave: "Even places like Club Kinetik expected guitars! I think I did a set one night and I didn't play any guitars, they were like, what the hell man, what's going on," says Loft in his deep dulcet radio tone. "I even grabbed the mic to apologise: next time, loads of guitars! That became a phrase."

From the Technodrome second room of Helter Skelter at the Sanctuary in Milton Keynes, with decks on chains swinging from the ceiling and sweat pouring down on the gurning harder harder ardkore Brits, Loftgroover emerged as one of the hardest and best-loved hardcore DJs of the '90s, doing things that nobody else would dare – like dropping undiluted metal into his nosebleed speedcore sets.

"At Helter Skelter, I'm dropping some metal, and this bouncer comes," Loft continues. "I don't know where he came from, and he goes to me, 'what the fuck are you doing? This is supposed to be a rave!' I've gone to him, 'mate, have a look down there'. And everyone was going absolutely fucking berserk metal," he laughs. "And just for him, I pull out this Napalm Death record, with 'Scum' on one side and 'You Suffer' on the other. I played one side, took the needle off, turned it over, and played the other side!"

One of the UK's greatest living DJs never intended to be a DJ. For Loft, the music itself was enough. "DJing didn't appeal to me," he says. "First and foremost, music to me is so personal. I'm really selfish about music. Once I'm in my thing, I don't really care what everyone else is doing." But Loft's all-consuming passion for the music that spoke "directly to his being" would also be his downfall: "Friends come and go, girlfriends come and go. The only thing that remains is your music. That's when everything stopped and gabber took over. Pow!"

Emerging with enviable mixing skills when beat-matching was rare, Lofty forged a career out of bucking trends and pioneering sonic pairings, from reggae 12"s mixed with hardcore rave, well before jungle, to premiering Belgian techno, bought straight from the source, to the breakbeat rave scene. He quickly had residencies at some of the best clubs in London, from South West techno crucible Knowledge to rave night Orange at North London's Rocket.

Wherever Lofty played, he made sure he stood out. "I was always into something different from my peers," he explains about growing up in the same West London district as Fabio and Grooverider, and Colin Dale (everyone would cross paths in the rave scene). "My subconscious wanted something else," he says. "A lot of DJs were playing for a rewind and I wasn't like that," he says about playing alongside DJs like Hype and Randall, and refusing to play the hits. "There was so much music out there that people were not hearing."

On June 4, 1994, Loftgroover landed in Paris for the inaugural Deep Of Darkness rave by promoter and DJ Armaguet Nad, where his mettle was tested over an eight hour back-to-back set with the Queen, Liza N Eliaz, "one of the coolest people ever," says Loft. "I'm sure they were giving out straightjackets at the door as you went in."

Connecting with the Russian renegade Rubick from Mad Dog Distribution, and hearing the scattergun speedcore of Parisian crew Gangstar Toons Industry set Loft on his own scarecore warpath when he returned home, playing across the megaraves of Scotland and the smaller, sweatier, exclusively hardcore club nights popping off nationwide, from Steam at the Downtown Club in Rhyl, North Wales, to the Shire Horse in St Ives, the legendary Cornish venue where Aphex Twin and Luke Vibert played their first sets.

Many metal-moshing raves later, by '98 Lofty's signature sound was catalogued on the critically acclaimed double mix CD, *Loftgroover Presents Speedcore*, which paired Rotterdam Records gabber and Industrial Strength hardcore techno with French speedcore and German terrorcore, mixed with undiluted metal towards the end. Alongside Earache bands like Morbid Angel and Brutal Truth, the release also featured a selection of Loft's own "thrash dance" hits, as Zeed and Agent Death, written together with his Scottish friend and collaborator, Vince Watson.

"We made loads of music together, most of which has never been released," Watson explains. "I didn't have a proper studio at the time, so we were literally recording on really poor equipment in my dining room." The handful of records they did release came out on Redhead Records, which was short-lived and just for fun. "I never considered myself to be a producer, so I didn't take it seriously, just had a laugh," says Loft. "And amazingly, people bought it."

Manu, meanwhile, was making his mark on the scene with his own landmark compilation, *Biomechanik*, which was just as musically discursive and well-received. Issued in '97 via Laurent Garnier's F Communications label, *Biomechanik Vol 1* reinforced Manu Le Malin's international status, not just a public figure in France and outspoken media personality, but also one of the country's most popular DJs, who helped turn around the media-seeded techno stigma in France. Packaged in Giger-inspired artwork with album-scope curation, featuring exclusive tracks sold off as EPs, Manu produced two editions of *Biomechanik* before the end of the decade.

It would take another six years for *Biomechanik Vol 3* to be released, which Manu issued just ahead of a burnout from touring – now as the band, Palindrome. Physically and mentally exhausted, crippled by gambling addiction and substance abuse, penniless and homeless and full of self-doubt, Manu self-exiled from music – and the rest of the world.

Back in Britain, Loftgroover was in crisis too. "I didn't want anything to do with music," he says. "I was surrounded by records. I couldn't get out of bed without stepping on records. I couldn't go shopping with the kids without people hailing me from buses. So one day I woke up and decided to get rid of every record that I owned, every single one."

His private pleasure was slipping away from him: "To see things blow up and then realise so much is wanted from you, it was like some kind of intrusion. The love I had for the music had turned into some kind of puppet show." And the music had changed beyond his control. "Gabber had lost its funkiness," he adds. "It had gone fast beyond reproach. It just wasn't the same."

On May 29, 1999, Loft played his last ever gabber-speedcore set for Helter Skelter. And even then, he almost didn't show. "I didn't want anything to do with music," says Loft. "I was the one that got the call," says Simon Underground, a friend of Loft's since the Knowledge club days, who helped turn Loft hardcore, and booked him for his Live Evil events. "He said, I'm putting it all in the fucking skip."

"The biggest mistake of my life was getting rid of those records," says Loft about the collection he had been building since primary school, with pocket money raised by helping his mum with the shopping. Ten weeks later, he returned to Helter Skelter for Energy '99, armed with a stack of other records to commit the "cardinal sin" of playing drum 'n' bass in the techno-purist Technodrome room. "People were shaking their fists," he recalls. "A couple wanted to fight with me. By that time, I'd had enough." He wasn't alone.

"It was end of the '90s, music was really changing, and I fucking had enough," says Industrial Strength's Lenny Dee. Darkness had descended upon the New York City rave scene. Manhattan rave haunt, The Limelight, was closed between '96 and '98, whilst owner Peter Gatien and Disco 2000 promoter Michael Alig were on trial for a DEA drug investigation and shocking murder scandal that the scene – and city – never ever recovered from.

Nightclubs, Downtown and Dirty ran the *Washington Post* in February, 1998, with a report from investigative journalist Frank Owen from the Gatien trial. "Gatien was acquitted earlier this week – mainly, it seems, because the government's case relied so heavily on the capricious testimony of thuggish drug dealers and professional partiers known as club kids," he wrote. "But Manhattan's famed downtown nightlife has not been exonerated; it emerged from the trial irrevocably tarnished."

Ketamine excess had replaced the ecstasy euphoria in NYC – a phenomenon that Owen was initially sent to cover for the Village Voice in 1995, as club overdoses kept hitting the media. Oliver Chesler turned his own experiences into the infamously salacious 'One Night in NYC' as The Horrorist, a track that had Pete Tong tell *Mixmag* in 2001: "Big records demand your attention, and this is bound to get yours [...] You could call it a date rape record but I think Oliver is taking the piss [...] Love it hate it, you will certainly know when you've heard it."

Paired with 'Mission Extacy' – a ride through the outer boroughs on a mission to get high – the record held a UV lamp to the decadent NYC Club Kid culture to reveal the seediness and sin amongst the heedless hedonism. "I went to the hospital for an ecstasy overdose," Chesler revealed to *El Garaje de Frank* magazine. "When I got back to my mother's home where I had a studio in the basement, I had a real sense of urgency in my head. I thought I would never go to a club again so I wanted to record what I saw there. With just a few pieces of gear (Mackie 1604, Roland TR-909, Shure SM58, Yamaha FB01) I recorded 'One Night in NYC.'"

The EP was issued in 1996, as Limelight's demagogue Club Kid, Michael Alig, was arrested for the brutal murder of his personal dealer Andre "Angel" Melendez. A few months later, tragedy directly struck the Industrial Strength family when DOA's Nicky Fingers died of a heroin overdose. The group had just issued their landmark *New York City Speedcore* album with Earache. "Once Nicky was gone, it was very hard to keep the energy level. It just wasn't the same in the studio," say Carl and Sal. "He was an inspiration, it was truly a lifestyle for him," adds Sal. "DOA was a three-person dynamic," says Carl. "When Nicky died, so did DOA. He lives on in every track."

"I had to take a serious break at that point," Lenny remarks. "I'd been going nonstop since the fucking '80s. I had to stop the label, I shut my studio down. I wasn't feeling any inspiration," he says. But the Brooklyn firecracker did not stay silent for long. As millennium bug doom ushered in the next decade of terror, the Industrial Strength engine was firing again on all cylinders, with new energy, a new sound, and a woman – Jules Separovic – at system control.

BE A FREAK
BE YOU

KEEP MOVING IN TIME

THREE FLOORS OF YOU, ASSAULT ART, HOUSE MUSIC SOUL FOOD, TELEVISION, AND YOUR FREINDS. AND ACID, AND VISUALS AND CHILL OUT ROOMS AND DRINKS AND MADNESS WITH A MESSAGE FOR ONE NIGHT ONLY.

SAT. NOV 17

12-8 uur

DJ'S: FIERCE RULING DIVA AND POSSE

PLANET E

FL 10-

LAST NIGHT DAMRAK 53

7

In a vacant factory where no Amsterdam hipsters dare to go, hard house and weirdo acid ricochets off the white-tiled slaughterhouse walls. This is a new kind of rave music, Lowlands grown, and just for these long haired gabbers who want it Harder! Faster! Louder! A short drive along the gritty Dutch coastline where a manmade island bristles with steel and smoking chimney stacks bulges into the North Sea, Holland's first big-tented dance event emits breakbeats and four-four kicks into the neon-orange polluted sky. It's not called gabber. For now it's rave, it's gabberhouse!

In the early '90s, Holland set the global standard for hardcore. This music united and divided raving communities worldwide, exported by a tiny nation six times smaller than the UK by "rival" record labels backed by major distribution networks. Dutch gabber was simultaneously pop music, in the charts, and for the boneheads only. In the Netherlands it quickly evolved from hyper-local outsider club scenes into a mainstream culture phenomenon, and one of the most significant subcultures of the era, equally feared and revered, with its own eye-catching uniform look of deceptively casual sportswear paired with an intimidating punk attitude.

But the roots of gabber – first described as gabberhouse – extend back to Amsterdam's Autumn of Love. As the trendy house music heads gathered at the RoXY rallying to the four-four rhythms of Eddy De Clercq, the freaks were gathering in the basement on the other side of the street, answering the queer call of Fierce Ruling Diva and their jackin' Lower East Side-meets-Amsterdam sound.

"We just took that spirit exactly how we experienced it in New York, and imported it to Amsterdam," explains Jeff "Abraxas" Porter, the DJ and voice of the Divas who turned Holland on to "serious Hardcore House" together with Dutch partner Jeroen Flamman, a post-punk drummer and the opposite of Jeff in almost every way. "That's why it worked," says Jeff. "And that's how we made all the songs as well," he says. "What he did for the songs and what I did was completely different."

From the summer of '88, inspired by their hormone-fueled nights together hopping from gay bar to club to loft party through the seedy boho district of Manhattan, Jeff and Jeroen returned to the Dutch party capital with a plan: "Dark hole club, low lights, DJ in back somewhere and just keep it fucking simple," says Jeff. "And you know, play real house music."

They started throwing parties at the DOK, a renowned gay discotheque on the Singel diagonally opposite to the RoXY. Jeff and Jeroen's events were free entry before midnight. As Amsterdam's Autumn of Love turned to Winter, they were selling out the place. Jeff started presenting his weekly radio show, *The Power Hour Of Dance Noise* on renowned Amsterdam pirate station Radio 100 (where he remained until 2000). Jeroen meanwhile started crafting their records, swapping his drum kit for a drum machine.

As Fierce Ruling Diva they wrote their first record, 'I Don't Wanna Be A Freak', a druggie inversion of Dynasty's '70s pop disco hit. This was about trawling for flesh, and not wanting to go to bed, and surrendering to your horny desires: "I don't wanna be a freak, but I can't help myself," as the lyrics ran, sung by Jeff. "It's horrible. I can't hear it," he exclaims decades later. "I don't like my voice. That's why I don't play my own tracks when I'm DJing at all. I always miss a beat or make a mistake, it's terrible."

They pressed 500 copies and self-released it the following summer, in August 1989. This was Holland's very first house 12" minting their label,

Lower East Side Records. "I was very much into the Chicago and New York sound," Jeff continues, recalling his first record – the *Chicago Trax Volume 1* double vinyl compilation from Trax Records – bought after dropping acid during a bus trip from Boston to New York whilst still a student. "I was very influenced by Farley "Jackmaster" Funk," he admits, "'I Don't Wanna Be A Freak' came from Europeanising him, or my interpretation of how it was going to work here [in Amsterdam]."

Then the iT club opened in September '89. With flamboyant transvestite hosts, fire eaters, and hunky topless males dancing in cages, the iT was a place to be seen, and even more exclusionary than the RoXY; where Jeff was welcomed, but Jeroen not. The duo realised they needed to take matters into their own hands. "We are very non-elitist, of course," says Jeff. "We weren't busy with money at all. Never was, and still not. It was all about the music."

Planet E evolved from private parties in Jeroen's apartment on the Damrak, aligned with the origins of New York disco and David Mancuso's fabled Loft parties, into raucous club nights on the Koggestraat, before moving onto a barge christened Subtopia, which was docked behind Centraal station.

This was the moment Dylan Hermelijn and Daniël (Dano) Leeflang plugged in their 303 and 606 drum machines and started jamming nonstop. "We were doing nothing but twisting knobs and playing records," Dano recalls in the first instalment of *VPRO*'s tryptic of films charting *30 Years of Dutch Dance*. "It was like living above an engine room," comments Dano's father Gerrit, "as if you were on a hundred-ton oil tanker, sailing across the street on the waves of house music."

In the Boudisque record store they handed Jeff and Jeroen one of their tapes, becoming the sludgy acid-electro 12", *The Sound Of Planet Earth* and the third release by Lower East Side Records, issued in 1990. Dano and Dylan played their first livesets together across Planet E and

Subtopia events, before Dano and Jeroen started up their own Monday club night – this time licensed – called Manic Monday at the Mazzo. They launched with bleep legends LFO playing live on September 23, 1991. Later guests included Eddie "Flashing" Fowlkes playing in '92, Lenny Dee at the start of his gabber phase in '93, and Jeff Mills in '94.

Amsterdam's tastemaking journalists were quick to damn this wilder house music culture, where everyone was welcome, no door bitches necessary. "He is the terror of fashionable Amsterdam and can spoil an evening of these chic nightclubbers," wrote Ardy Beesemer – a DJ at the RoXY – in a series of critical articles for music magazine *Oor*, between the summer and autumn of '91. "He is omnipresent and loves beer with a few pills. He dresses badly, has a bad haircut and dances as stiff as a Ninja Turtle. His taste is anything but sophisticated and maybe that's why he loves house so much (just like mundane clubland). It's the GABBER!"

"Gabber is an Amsterdam Yiddish slang word," explains Ilja Reiman, Amsterdam's "first" gabber. "People from the RoXY called us this as a swear name: the gabbers are not allowed in. And we said, fine, we are the gabbers. We embraced the name."

The illegal rave, Multigroove, was his rowdy rebuttal, launched as a friendly neighbourhood "demolition party" at the De Wielingen schoolhouse squat in August '91. In the daytime there was a BBQ and a cover band playing songs by the Beatles, with the downstairs old gym serving as the main stage. By nightfall the street was suddenly blocked with vehicles: shuttle buses leading a procession of cars, mopeds, bicycles. The real party kicked off.

Seven months of roving raves followed, playing cat and mouse with the police, before Multigroove moved into the Elementenstraat in the industrial West of the city in April 1992. The unforgiving tiles that lined the walls made the acoustics sound terrible. There was just a single main hall, which they divided into two with speakers. But over a run of 61 unlicensed parties held across consecutive weekends, here Amsterdam gabberhouse hardened into hardcore. Multigroove's Elementenstraat residents included Jeroen and Jeff, DJing separately as Flamman and Abraxas, Dano playing live acid sets, and Dov the Prophet, before these two shot to stardom.

Where Amsterdam's early gabbers were relegated to squatted barges and illegal warehouses on the outskirts of town, in Rotterdam they were freely gathering in iconic nightclubs throughout Holland's harbour city. Bombed flat during the war and in constant renewal, Rotterdam resounded with the rhythmic metal clang of foundations perpetually being laid and the constant shuffling of trainered feet. Within the dungeon-like bowels of a 1900s stately villa, nestled in the shadow of the city's most recognisable landmark, the Euromast, a harder-edged form of dance music evolved that would define Rotterdam, worldwide, for decades.

"Parkzicht was our Haçienda," says Rob Fabrie, AKA Waxweazle. "It was hard-edged because of the Rotterdam spirit: we are not bullshitting around." The original Parkzicht sound was eclectic, with residents Ricky da Dragon playing mellow at one end, and DJ Rob with his three decks and 909 at the other, pushing a harder and more distorted style on Friday nights. In the parking lot, bouncers sold bootleg cassette tapes to gabbers not ready to go home. Inside, the dancefloor was encircled by stairs sweeping up to a circular viewing platform. It was loud and hellish for the uninitiated – heaven for the heads. Bass-heavy music spilled across the streets, causing complaints and neighbourly friction that would escalate into the '90s – along with the music.

"We listened to hard beat, a sound that was coming from the new beat generation in Belgium," Fabrie explains, "Robert Amani was very influential, and hard hip hop, like Silver Bullet '20 Seconds To Comply', that was a Parkzicht anthem, and breakbeats."

Parkzicht was not a "gabber cave", insists Paul Elstak in *VPRO*'s *30 Years of Dutch Dance*, but he did bring gabber into the club: "They played good house music. But at the end of the night, seven or eight in the morning, we hit the gas," he admits.

Before Elstak became synonymous with Rotterdam's straight-to-the-point style of hardcore gabber music, powered by distorted kick drums and fiery, provocative lyrics (aligned with the gnarliest hardcore techno from Frankfurt troupe PCP), Paul was spinning hip hop at the BlueTiek-In, Rotterdam's first super disco, and working behind the counter of the Mid-Town Records store on the Nieuwe Binnenweg.

Fabrie connected with Paul when he was just seventeen, making their first hip house record together with Richard van Naamen as Holy Noise in 1990. The group broke through one year later, sporting matching blockhead haircuts and mustaches, with their ravey sample-heavy hit 'James Brown Is Still Alive' – a hip hop-styled battle response to L.A. Style's 'James Brown Is Dead', which was flying off the shelves at the time.

If the sound of Amsterdam was more acid-driven, experimental and eclectic, the club sound of Rotterdam was industrial, industrious, and naturally hardcore; a symphony of the working class city itself. The Parkzicht crowd was underground and working class: a mix of labourers and dock workers, football supporters and topless guys draped in python snakes or wearing chainmail. "Everyone, welcome, do whatever you want. No door bitches," says Rob Christensen, another Rotterdam teen who joined the gabber scene through selling records on Saturdays from the Mid-Town shop with Paul. "That's why sneakers and sportswear were also worn," he explains, "because in Amsterdam you needed to wear shirts and be fashionable. In Rotterdam it was: don't be fashionable, be yourself."

The sports look was practical but also a reaction to the sleek aesthetics courted by the "mellow" house scene, which gabber was diametrically opposed to. "In Amsterdam discotheques, when you arrived the doorman would look at you, what kind of shoes you're wearing, are you keeping up with the fashion of the day," Ilja confirms, now bearded but still with his youthful mane. "At Multigroove, you didn't have to put on shiny shoes or go to the barber. The real gabbers had long hair, dressed in nice white shirts."

This founding gabberhouse scene was separate to techno, although techno was influential in Rotterdam, where a thriving techno subculture evolved early on around the Clone Records store, pioneering hardware producers like Speedy J, releasing on the Stealth Records label and Plus 8 label (straddling Windsor and Detroit). At Parkzicht, Plus 8 tracks like Cybersonik's 'Thrash' and the instrumental 'Thrash Beats' were pitched up on hacked turntables during the Friday's hardcore closing hours. "We took it up a notch," says Fabrie. "We opened the SL-1200 and we turned up the pitch so it gets two times as fast. And then people started to play way above 200 BPM. I wasn't really into that," he adds.

The Plus 8 co-founders' encounter with Holland's football-chanting gabbers at Parkzicht on November 6, 1992 has been well documented as the turning point for Richie Hawtin to begin developing his introspective Plastikman alias, and for John Acquaviva's move into house. Less known is resident DJ Rob's tireless efforts to keep hooliganism – and its antisemitic slurs – away from his dancefloor.

"For the audience inside, the party turns into a nightmare the moment Janssen turns down the volume knob. According to him, this has happened four times in recent months, each time because part of the audience rhythmically began to chant the cry 'Jews, Jews' originating from football stadiums," reported the *NRC* newspaper from December 5, 1992. "We want to pay attention to these kinds of things before they get out of hand," was Janssen's response. "Those boys usually react very calmly," he explained to *NRC*. "They understand it, you just have to really rub their noses in it."

"Rave became hardcore in a matter of months. Every week it was harder and harder," says Ilja who says that by '93 the drive towards harder and faster tracks was already getting out of hand. "Multigroove is multi grooves, open minded, everything should be able to happen; not any more."

On Saturday May 15, 1993, Multigroove's reign at Elementenstraat ended in a violent police raid as part of an undercover operation, codenamed *Operation Ponytail.* All Multigroove founders and DJs performing that night were arrested – including Jeff Abraxas. Ilja was imprisoned for four weeks and fined 1.5 million guilders (around €770,000) and the Elementenstraat was forced to close for good. Vigil-raves were held outside the venue for two weeks afterwards by Multigroove's devoted community.

"Then gabber was a lifestyle," Iljia concludes. For thousands of troubled kids across the Lowlands, gabber was much more than that. It was life.

E
U
R
O

R
A
V
E
#
3

RIGE
presents

D.J.'s / ACTS

JOEY BELTRAM
WESTBAM
PAUL ROTTERDAM RECORDS
ROTTERDAM NATION
80 AUM SURPRISE
MAC DE HEY
FAME DANCERS

100kw BOOM BOOM SOUND!!!
MASSIVE LIGHTS AND
EUROLASER!!!

PRESALE-PRICE ƒ 30.-

19 december 1992

ENERGIEHAL
ROTTERDAM

HARD SCORE

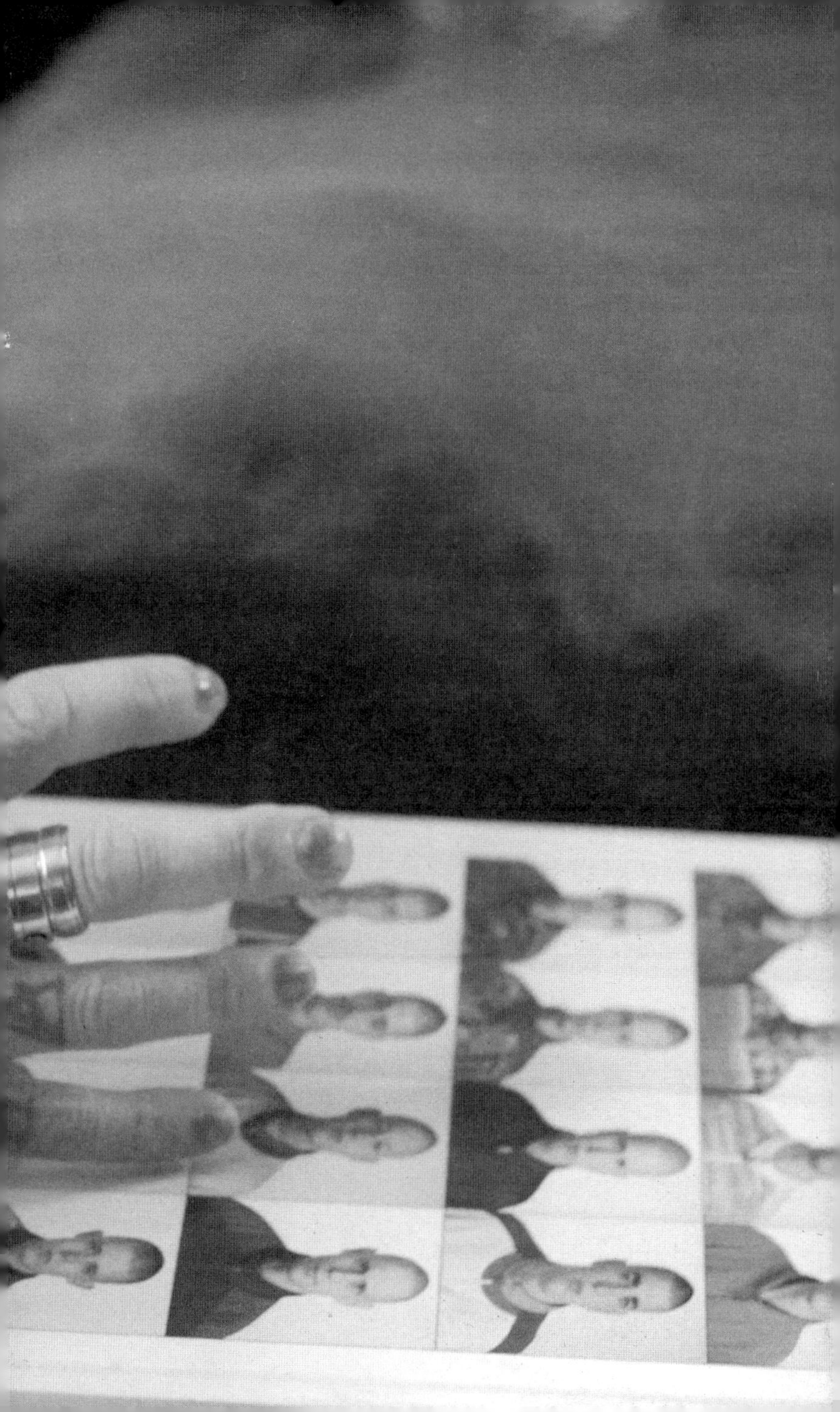

8

"Gabbers. First impressions: They are aggressive and racist," begins a typical Dutch TV news special from 1996. "They wear tracksuits from expensive brands. And they all do drugs. Whoever encounters them in the street is best to cross to the other side."

"Why isn't anyone writing about the camaraderie of gabbers?" said one frustrated reader in a letter to national newspaper *De Volkskrant*, the same year. "I hope that for once you let an article be written by someone who really understands it. In other words: a real gabber!"

Gabbers were ostracised and largely misunderstood by those outside the subculture. But those who were in, were in it all the way. Gabbers were a great source of fascination for newspapers and TV journalists covering the craze that had claimed one in three of its youngsters during gabber's peak through the mid-'90s, when even primary school kids were shaving their heads bald, and chopping and gurning in the wild folkish gestures of the hakke dance, in big hall raves and tiny youth centres throughout the country.

The gabber subculture provided a home for those who didn't have one, and beyond your gabbers nothing else mattered. "It's not a way of life, it is my life," states original gabber Leonie Neervoort. "People would always look at you differently. You're a girl, but you're half-shaven," she says, referring to the classic gabber undercut worn by girls in this period, which she adopted from school. "You're making a statement. You're different from others. And I think you have to be brave to do that, especially back then."

Leonie is one of the most well-documented gabbers from Rotterdam, and the first "Gabberbitch" in photographer Ari Versluis' iconic tiled street style photo series of girl gabbers from 1996. Snapped outside of a rave in Vlaardingen when she was still in her teens, you can see her blond hair tied back in blue, white and red bands, revealing the classic gabber undercut and ears choked in gold rings. "I still know a lot of them," she says about the other girls in the series, "and they're all still raving."

Leonie went to her first gabber rave when she was just fourteen years old, she's been a gabber ever since. For gabbers, this raving subculture was a much-needed escape from reality, a physical and psychological relief from the daily grind: "In the past a lot of gabbers had problems and a lot of shit," she explains. Leonie went to Parkzicht first before discovering Rotterdam's gabber temple, the Energiehal, and "after that it was only rave, rave, rave!" She recalls her first Energiehal experience, back in 1992, as though she was there only last week: "You had the prickles [goosebumps] as soon as you went into the hall and felt the bass. You only had the hall, some stroboscope, and the music. No expensive laser shows and all that shit. It was my second home."

The Energiehal was a disused sports hall in Rotterdam West, seized by self-described "business DJ" and promoter George Ruseler in the winter of '92. Ruseler would occupy this 15,000 capacity venue until its demolition for a carpark in 1999, building a loyalist Rotterdam following from his gabber party, Megarave. Ruseler's live act, Rotterdam Terror Corps, featuring longtime friend MC Raw and a roving troupe of female stripshow dancers, were the Megarave houseband. "Harder, softer, darker, grittier. Always in the opposite direction than others, that became our trademark," as he explained to Rotterdam *Gers! Magazine*. The Dark Twins – fronted by the two MCs Cyriel Brandon and Remondo Sedoc (AKA Dart) – were popular residents, playing up to the Megarave's later theatrics, like the time they electrocuted each other live on stage.

Sporthallen Zuid was Amsterdam's gabber temple, with its three big halls and warren of smaller rooms, connected by red locker-lined corridors to get lost in, and dancefloors slicked with sweat. Hellraiser with its haunting 80s fantasy-horror mascot, Pinhead, was Amsterdam's iconic gabber rave, which moved into Sporthallen Zuid in early '93. Hellraisers played up to the scene's video nasty aesthetics, like the edition Pinhead took out a buzzsaw and chopped off the leg of a raver, as women seductively wrestled in the pools of blood left behind. This was total unbridled raving freedom, and Rotterdam was welcomed too, with DJ Rob and Paul Elstak booked for the early editions.

But these were also discrete and separate gabber scenes, formed from two city rivals locked in a cultural battle going back centuries; which was animated and embodied from the first proper Rotterdam gabber record.

"The war started because of that *VPRO* television show," says Rob Fabrie about the 1991 *VPRO* youth culture TV program, *Onrust,* that tried to explain this new house music phenomenon: "This is the essence of gabberhouse: Bam Bam Bam Bam, and doing this with your head," said Amsterdam artist D-Shake, whilst bobbing like a pigeon. "It comes from football supporters," he added, "Girls don't like it at all."

Rob Fabrie co-wrote the first – and most iconic – Dutch gabber diss record when he was an angry teenager, although he has never claimed to be a gabber himself. "I think gabber is a shitty term," he insists. "It always leaves a bad taste in my mouth, the whole gabber thing." He elaborates: "Gabber started as a name to diss the music that we made in Rotterdam. I know it means 'friend', but I still remember why they said it, and so I'm always saying I'm hardcore."

Amsterdam Waar Lech Dat Dan? (Amsterdam, where is that then?)

launched Rotterdam records with controversy in April 1992 – the same week Multigroove moved into the Elementenstraat. Cartoonist Linia's cheeky Euromaster character adorns the cover, destroying Amsterdam in a spray of golden piss. *Gabber z'in is géén schande!* (There's no shame in being a gabber!) is written across its urine-yellow vinyl sticker with "blah blah blah blah blah..." serving as liner notes scrawled across the back. It looks like a gimmick, and has become one with time, but this record was written from a place of genuine fury. "We were angry about one article in the *Nieuwe Revu* magazine," explains Fabrie. "They stated that the harder house came from Amsterdam, and we were like, fuck that!"

The record's titular track was Rotterdam's barbed response, lifting its distorted end of days rumbling from PCP's 'We Have Arrived'. 'F..K DJ Murderhouse' on the B-side was his "angry bedroom demo" against the Amsterdam critic Ad de Feijter, who "trashed" Fabrie's first group, Holy Noise, in a review for *Disco Dance* magazine under the pen name DJ Murderhouse. "He thought they were absolutely awful and I got mad because yeah, I was young. I was stupid," says Fabrie.

'Rotterdam Éch Wel!' completes the three track debut EP from Rotterdam Records, featuring Fabrie as the voice of this typical Rotterdam expression, roughly translated as: We are Rotterdam; the label's potent statement of intent. They called themselves Euromasters in homage to the Euromast that towered over the club where Rotterdam gabber culture gestated.

Just like PCP in Frankfurt, Rotterdam Records built its own music world, and raving community. Its releases were by and for Rotterdammers, and held a mirror to Dutch society and its own gabber culture, with a barbed Rotterdam tongue firmly in cheek. Sperminator's 'No Women Allowed' pokes at the "sexists" media stereotypes (when there were as many girl gabbers as boys, especially in Rotterdam); but it also makes light of its own gabber boys-only club, where there were no women producers, and very few women DJs for much of the '90s.

In 'Rotterdam Subway', General Noise plots a gabber's journey from Zuidplein to Rotterdam Centraal heading on a night out, the fidgety drum machine emulating the amphetamine anticipation. Rotterdam's main station in the early '90s was also a notorious spot for junkies, who gathered here – from all over the country – for the free methadone clinic at Perron Null, initiated by Reverend Visser of the Pauluskerk in 87. Perron Null was a scourge on Rotterdam's image – a city already damned as dangerous – and a blight on the taxi drivers who worked there. The issue came to a head during the European Football Championship in the summer of '92, when a group of around 100 marines in training from the Rotterdam van Ghent barracks showed up with the intention to clear all junkies from the station. Shortly after, Rotterdam Records released *Rotterdam Subway*, with the A2 track 'Drugs (Perron 0)' in winking tribute.

Humour was at the heart of Rotterdam gabber, and Euromasters were the living, breathing, laughing embodiment of the laddish culture, which loved football and playing stupid pranks (*Hardscore*), liked to fuck ('Noiken In Die Koiken' from *Oranje Boven*) but also fuck things up (*Alles Naar De Kl--te*). Rob Fabrie only contributed to the first Euromasters record, the rest were written by whoever was in the studio with Paul at the time. But the group has always been fronted by the same pair of unlikely friends: the more serious gabber Rob Christensen, and the self-confessed "clown" Fabian Kruizinga. Whilst Rob C worked with Paul at the Mid-Town Records store, Fabian came from the house scene and worked with Tiësto and Ferry Corsten at Basic Beat – another record store located on the Nieuwe Binnenweg.

When they were first asked to be the Milli Vanilli of Euromasters, neither expected much of it: "It was for fun, we thought they'd only make one track," says Fabian. They performed their first Euromasters show on May 22, 1992, part of a Mid-Town Records party at Tomorrowland, a spectacular domed nightclub spread over five floors in South Rotterdam that looked like the inside of a spaceship. "When we started the record people went completely mad," recalls Rob C. "We were just standing there, it didn't matter what we did, and the crowd went totally crazy. It didn't even last fifteen minutes."

"We had stupid glasses, we were supposed to look funny because we thought it was fun," says Fabian. But there was another reason for the disguise: "We didn't want to be recognisable," he confesses.

They elevated the playback DAT show, prevalent at the time, to an art, and often on the fly. Rob C recalls another early Rotterdam show at the Copacabana: "A guy came up to us, and he was like: this keyboard doesn't have any cables. We said it was 'infrared'. Wi-Fi didn't exist," he laughs. "After that, every gig I played I took some cables with me, and made a show of laying them all out with tape."

Shows have remained wild and unpredictable, with the pair sometimes playing an accordion – or a dildo. "I don't feel any shame on stage, and that's why people like it," says Fabian. Euromasters were not a serious act – but the intention behind the music was. "It's not a parody," Rob C is keen to clarify. "We're not making fun of it, we are having a fun approach to it, that's the difference. And we take it seriously."

But despite playing all over the world, including a tour through Japan in '98, in the Netherlands Euromasters have always been a strictly regional act. They only ever played one major show in Amsterdam, back in 1993, representing Rotterdam Records at the European Dance Music Convention (an early iteration of Amsterdam Dance Event) at an event aptly named Unity: the party without borders. "We didn't play 'Amsterdam Waar Lech Dat Dan,'" says Rob Christensen, "only Rotterdam-pro, instead of anti-Amsterdam."

Euromasters were defined by their first record and its embedded Amsterdam-Rotterdam rivalry, but the gimmick was more seriously adopted by the gabber subculture when it got irreversibly mixed up with football. "We underestimated the football rivalry," admits Dennis Copier, teenage DJ star of Pompeï, a 250-capacity youth centre in the south of the city, and the only club that played hardcore from the beginning to the end. Just like the UK rave movement, gabber was a dance culture for everyone, and all were welcome, but where the brutal football hooliganism melted in the ecstasy rush in Britain, or was left at the door at least, feuding Dutch football fans brought their violent division to the gabber halls.

Euromasters' fourth and final EP, *Hardscore*, a parody on the 1994 World Cup, fatally unified the group with its gabber-hooligan culture; its 'Oprottûh (Hooligans Mix)' featuring roaring football crowd samples hid behind a satirical veneer that was just too close to the truth. "By *Hardscore* we were trying to find a subject to make a song about, instead of it coming from the heart," says Rob C, "I think that was the reason we stopped with Euromasters."

Gabber acts might have played up the feud, but the football rivalry was no joke. Following a series of escalated events, by the mid-'90s Rotterdam didn't go to Amsterdam anymore, and Amsterdam was not welcomed in Rotterdam.

HAPPY BOUNCY MENTAL

W.A.P. Productions Presents

Friday Januari 19th

Hellway to Mokum

DANOCHOSENFEW**ABRAXAS**
REMSY**JEROEN FLAMMAN**
LIVE ON STAGE
PARTY ANIMALS

Mister and Misses Gabber Contest

De Valk IJplein 3 Amsterdam Noord

Entree f 20,- Doors open 21.00 till.......

9

By 1994 the gabber scene was in crisis. Sensationalised (and often inaccurate) news reports of vandalism, violence and drug overdoses at gabber raves rippled through the Dutch media, triggering a national moral panic. Local governments in major gabber cities like Rotterdam and Utrecht were provoked to rescind licenses for gabber events, or limit the number of gabber raves. According to *De Groene Amsterdammer* magazine in an article (published November 27, 1996) the Dutch parliament even called for a complete ban on all large gabber raves.

Christian Evangelist teams in their iconic red "Jesus buses" had joined the media crews picketing outside the big gabber halls; one group trying to save these poor souls, the other to damn them. Hellraiser in Amsterdam hit the headlines after an event at Sporthallen Zuid on September 3 resulted in eight visitors hospitalised, reports *De Groene Amsterdammer*, after ingesting ecstasy containing a "life-threatening dose of MDEA". One month later, on November 21, *NRC Handelsblad* covered a gabber rave at Rotterdam gabber temple the Energiehal, opening with "a bald gabber" cheerfully waving to local TV crews after being stabbed in the back with a filed-down toothbrush, before detailing a series of drug-related deaths at "house parties" across the nation.

"Now they want everybody to believe that we were kind of hippies in the past and that's really, really not true," confirms Energiehal raver Leonie.

"It was not all love, peace and happiness. There were a lot of fights in the past; a lot of fights."

"By 1994, the music was too hard, too fast. Fewer girls were dancing, and we lost the party atmosphere," Paul Elstak explains to Simon Reynolds in *Generation Ecstasy*. "And kids were taking too many drugs to keep up with the speed." Rebranding as "DJ Paul", Rotterdam's gabber godfather turned to the singalong, saccharine pop music of happy hardcore, as panacea for the crisis.

DJ Paul's first hit, 'Luv U More', was a club remix of British pop group Sunscreem (who scored a hit with the original version in 1992). Paul's version was sung by vocalist Shaydie, and came with a promotional video of the pair on tour, featuring Paul's own daughter sweetly miming along to the words. The record came with a message: "If you're gonna use drugs, be careful! Stop hurting yourselves and the hardcore scene!"

'Luv U More' peaked at number 2 in the Dutch charts on July 1, 1995; a winning formula for parent label Mid-Town Records, which was repeated over commercially successful follow-ups 'Rainbow In The Sky', 'Rave On' and 'The Promised Land', all ghost-produced by Paul's Mid-Town Records colleague, Koen Groeneveld, AKA The Ultimate Seduction.

Happy hardcore popularised and polarised the Dutch gabber scene. It brought founding gabber artists like Paul, and the Fierce Ruling Divas as Party Animals for Mokum (Amsterdam's answer to Rotterdam Records), into the Dutch charts, and with it a whole new wave of fans. But happy hardcore, or Dutch happy gabber, also had a darker, more sinister side. And the most neurotic came from the ruffneck port city of Rotterdam, from Patrick van Kerckhoven's Acen-indebted DJ Ruffneck alias and his breakbeat-driven "artcore" sound.

As Paul became the pop face of happy hardcore, he was simultaneously slinging harder-hitting breakbeat-gabber records, together with Mid-Town Records shop protegees Lars Tindal and Dennis Copier (AKA DJ Panic) as The Forze DJ Team. On the cover of their '94 debut record, *May The Forze Be With You* (for Forze Records), the trio are depicted as laughing Forze bears: Lars with his foppish curtain hairdo, Dennis Panic with his blond slickback, and "Daddy" Paul in the centre with his moustache and golden techniques on a chain. But these aren't your typical cutesy *knuffel* toys. Designed by Rotterdam graffiti artist Slush, on merch the Forze bear mascot is depicted hiding hand grenades and guns behind its back beneath the strapline, Wanna Play? with a cheeky-evil grin across its fuzzy face.

The music was just as dichotic: pairing the hard-edge four-four gabber sound of Rotterdam, as in 'Step The Fuck Off', with happy bouncy funcore, like 'Sweat On My Balls'; both from the inaugural Forze EP. As with Euromasters, the Forze project reflected Rotterdam's party culture, which was steeped in very real danger, serving as colourful distraction for one of the most violent and divided times in the gabber scene. And it wasn't all football-related. In 1996, Parkzicht was forced to close by Rotterdam city mayor Bram Peper following a series of gang-related shootings inside the club; ten years earlier, BlueTiek-In – Paul's first DJ residency – had made headlines in another club shooting, resulting in the death of an eighteen-year-old visitor and twenty-one-year-old doorman.

Happy hardcore signified Dutch rave's transition from a fringe renegade youth movement into mainstream pop culture. And as gabber's popularity grew, it became an exploitable commodity for advertisers wanting to cash in on the craze. Gabber culture was used to sell a range of products, from dip sauce to Kit Kats, as the music was in the process of selling out, too.

'I Wanna Be A Hippy' is one of the biggest, certainly most divisive gabber-pop records of all time. Originally written by British husband-and-wife act Technohead (behind plenty more caustic and experimental fare as GTO), the Flamman & Abraxas remix for Mokum sold 50,000 copies at home, earning it gold and silver awards in Holland, Germany and the UK. None of the remixers, including Dano, earned any royalties from the release (after waiving their rights in a swap deal). But the gabber-pop act that emerged from the remix did become one of the most successful Dutch dance acts of all time.

Party Animals were the Euromasters of Amsterdam – admit the Euromasters frontmen. They were a satirical act fronted by real Amsterdam gabbers who regularly partied at Amnesia, the Amsterdam city centre gabber club from Jeff and Jeroen after Subtopia and Multigroove were shut down by police. The group scored a series of number one hits for the Mokum label between February ('Have You Ever Been Mellow?') and August ('Aquarius') 1996. But satirical success tipped into parody over follow-up acts like Hakkûhbar with their hit 'Gabbertje' which went to the top of the Dutch charts in the weeks leading up to Christmas, and stayed in the top 10 for 8 weeks.

"The real damage was done by 'Gabbertje,'" says Rob Fabrie, who turned to making darker, more neurotic happy hardcore as Waxweazle in the mid-'90s after quitting Holy Noise. "All those stupid records like 'my grandma is a gabber' or something. All that bullshit. That really led to the death of happy hardcore."

Written by ex-punk frontman Bob Fosko as Hakkûhbar, signed to Mokum major label parent Roadrunner, 'Gabbertje' was a gabberised cover of the 1960s children's TV show *Swiebertje* and inspired a series of spin-off parody acts targeting a kiddy audience performing at kids gabber raves – real gabber raves with gabber DJs, but for school kids – through '97, as Dutch gabber pride turned to shame and ridicule.

Lads line the barriers inside the tent, becoming a wall of torsos with arms triple-striped in Adidas, knuckles clenched around glowsticks. "BRING ON THE GABBER!" they yell over the deafening banshee-din of whistles, "LENNY DEEEEEEE! GABBER UP YER ARSE!" Behind this barricade of human excitement, ravers jog on the spot as the day's last rays of light seep through the tarp. They've been led on site, past the flashing bumper cars and steaming food stalls, by a traditional Highland Pipe Band dressed in white spats, red kilts and black feather bonnets. And now they're ready to let rip at the craziest rave in tartan technoland.

"In my worst nightmare, I've been kidnapped by a bunch of tartan techno nutters," wrote Jim Byers in Scottish free mag, *The List*, in August 1996 as the city center superclubber was preparing to attend his first Rezerection: "hardcore rave hell."

Through the second half of the '90s, Dutch and Scottish hardcore rave scenes twinned in playful happy gabber music and public ridicule. In Scotland, this played out across the big tops of Rezerection, held at the Royal Highland Showground on the outskirts of Edinburgh.

At the Event 2, held on July 30 in 1994, happy gabber from Rotterdam and hardcore techno from the South of England converged with Industrial Strength beats from Brooklyn; the summer banging gabber kicks fused with piano-riffy rave, produced from the machine-laden home studio of Scott Brown. This regional hardcore sound, christened bouncy techno, ranged from the happy hardcore silliness of 'Toy Town' by Hixxy & Sharkey to the Ruffneck classic 'Jiiieehaaaa' (by Diss Reaction) – according to Scottish rave bible *M8* magazine and their '95 *Bouncy Techno Anthems* compilation.

Bouncy techno was fun, and it banged. But behind this unashamed party music, Godfather Scott Brown was a serious studio nerd. He formed his first rave band Q-Tex in 1991 with classmate Gordon Anderson whilst studying physics at Glasgow Caledonian. He had been messing around with keyboards since his teens and loved playing live; DJing looked boring. When Q-Tex signed to Glasgow institution 23rd Precinct Recordings, they became one of the brightest stars of the Scottish hardcore rave scene, adding singer Gillian Tennant to perform their cheesier Europop hits, like 'Believe' and 'Power of Love'.

But the group also had a darker side. "We've always split the music

50/50 with hardcore and commercial stuff," Scott explains in their 1995 VHS promo, *Q-Tex – So Far*: "When we started out, we never wanted to get into the charts at all. We were playing the worst hostels, the worst pubs, you name it, we've done it. Taking 50 quid here, 100 pound there" – and spending all the gig money on petrol to get to the next show. "But at the end of the day it's a business, you want to make a professional career out of this," he admits in the film, "we've got to make some money, let's go for some chart success."

By '96, Scott Brown had self-released his debut album, *The Theory Of Evolution*, and was facing off with Billy Bunter on the Rezerection label. Close your eyes and Scott Brown sounded like gabber on the Rez mainstage, but open them and you'd be surrounded by white gloves and glowsticks, giant inflatable penises, with lads furiously cross-stepping in plaid pyjamas on stage next to women who were ribbon dancers, instead of strippers.

"Light sticks windmilling from podiums. White gloves smeared with Vicks vapour rub. Happy faces covered in orange and green dayglo body paint. While all these things would normally have made us wince and look the other way in embarrassment, at Rezerection no one gave a monkey's," as Rez veteran Thom Dibdin wrote in *The List* from August '96. "We didn't give a monkey's about them either. Because Rezerection gave us the freedom to do exactly what we wanted to do."

Rez was spectacle-driven and spectacular from the first edition, featuring rescued movie sets to recreate the pyramids of Egypt, or the fanfare of a circus with aerialists and fire jugglers included. By Event 5, held on August 24, 1996, two tents had expanded into five arenas, covering the wide range of raving music tribes, from the London Acid Techno warehouse punk of Chris & Aaron Liberator, to Metalheadz drum 'n' bass from Kemistry & Storm, to the purist Detroit techno soul of Juan Atkins, Kevin Saunderson and Kenny Larkin. It was also one of its last big Rez events before the Scottish rave scene burned itself out.

After the '94 boom, by '96 hardcore in Scotland was dwindling. "Not due to any lack of popularity," as *i-D* magazine reported that summer: "The record labels are flourishing, the DJs booked for months in advance. The clubs, though, are closing." Journalist Bethan Cole noted that there were only "a handful of hardcore venues left" as others were moving into house music, to rebrand from the tartan techno nutter image. "All the venue owners want to do house now, because there's this feeling that they don't want to be associated with the image of the ridiculous Scottish raver," stated Jamie Raeburn from Clubscene Records, "y'know, all big staring eyes. I mean, nobody wants to be associated with that any more."

The boom and bust of Scottish hardcore was threaded by a series of high-profile ecstasy overdoses, all connected to one club: Hangar 13, the self-billed Hardest Club in the World at the Ayr Pavilion on the East coast. Nineteen-year-old Andrew Dick and eighteen-year-old John Nisbet died the same night, twenty-year-old Andrew Stoddart died three months later. *Hanger 13 and the Dance with Death* ran Scottish paper *The Herald* in February 1995. The tragedies pushed new event licensing laws through the Scottish parliament, which became law in '96, mandating chill-out areas with freely available water, and paramedics on standby.

"Hangar 13 was everywhere in the media," says hardcore raver-turned-promoter David "Boony" Brownlie, "but Fubar had a strong relationship with the licensing board and were able to prove they had the infrastructure to prevent anything like that happening there. We were lucky," he adds.

The Fubar (short for Fucked Up Beyond All Recognition) in Stirling was Scotland's premier hardcore rave club, and one of the few venues with a late license. "It was all-nighters, twelve hours of madness every week for the next four or five years," adds Martin Langer AKA DJ Obsession, who took over the bookings from 1995 with his Inner Rhythm night, which kicked off with firecracker Lenny Dee and Rotterdam's breakbeat champion Ruffneck Alliance.

"It was absolute mayhem in there, everybody fucked up sweating and fucking steam coming off them," says Boony, who grew up on the Fubar's doorstep. "I'd go there religiously. I was a manager at McDonald's, giving everybody free burgers – and I was getting free tickets to all these events," he laughs.

"I would go into McD's and order a burger and walk out with five happy meals," adds Martin, who became involved in the Fubar by accident, filling in for one of the DJs who didn't show up one night: "I wasn't old enough to be there," he adds. "I was underage, but I had my big brother's ID so I was alright."

Fubar started hosting all-nighters in late '92. A discotheque since the 80s with big wooden doors leading into a wide corridor lit up in red, on the ground floor, the old canteen was converted into a record store that Martin presided over, open every Tuesday til the weekend party kicked off. There was another lounge area downstairs with a bar and pool tables, which opened on Friday and Saturday before the club nights. The main dancefloor was upstairs and packed out most weekends.

Martin's Inner Rhythm night brought the harder sound of Europe and America to this quiet market town surrounded by farmland. But it took a while for the bouncy techno ravers to get this "nosebleed" side of hardcore rave. "A lot of people were put off by gabber," admits the promoter that brought Disciples of Annihilation to the UK for the first time. "We got offered DOA as part of the deal with Rob Gee" – the Limelight gabber-rockstar, and producer of the Industrial Strength hit 'Gabber Up Your Ass', which was big in Scotland at the time. "Because nobody had ever heard of DOA before, we made a big song and dance about it on the flyer."

"But they messed up the flyer and put Nasenbluten on it," adds Boony of the other Industrial Strength group making noise in 1995, signed from Newcastle Australia with their cheapcore album debut, *100% No Soul Guaranteed*. Boony recalls that messy Inner Rhythm night from April

1995, when NYC's outer boroughs invaded medieval Scotland: "The vibe inside the club was always superb, everybody was always up for it there, but people were drifting out saying 'that was too mental!'"

"These guys had never left New York before, and they got absolutely mangled," adds Martin. "Then Sal [Mineo] realised the American power outlet was different to the UK, and they didn't have a converter to plug in a sampler or any of his equipment. Loads went wrong that night."

"The Scotland tour was just insanity," say DOA's Carl and Sal, recalling the Fubar crowd "slamming the guard rail up and down while losing it to 'Extreme Gangsta.'"

Despite the loyalist community that grew between the record store and Inner Rhythm nights, typified by diehards like Boony, Fubar ended suddenly in the Spring of '97, just as Rez held its final megarave. On March 29, the Fubar hosted its final sweaty rager – and it was a happy hardcore night.

"I remember that day," says Boony sadly. "I walked in and asked Martin, 'what's coming up?' He said, 'I don't know how to tell you this: that's it, it's finished.' And my world fell apart."

EMBER 1994. ISSUE No. 68. PRICE £1.60
TLAND. N. IRELAND. EIRE. NORTH OF ENGLAND
SELECTED DISTRIBUTION IN CENTRAL LONDON

M8

REACTIVE BASS

The Final drugs warning!

plus our weekend tribute to JAMES McCABE at the Metro

Believe in the Power of

Q-TEX

"Raving is about dancing, not drugs"

9 770954 689033

TERRORCORE

BUNKER SPEZIAL

SYLVESTER

31.12.92 2100cet

DJ's	Roland	
	Rolf	
	Motte	
	Spezial	
	Cut-X	
Live on air		
	Loopzone	(Berlin)
	Dr. Motte	(Debut)
	Mark N-R-G	(Overdrive)
	XOL-Dog 400	(MCP-Gesandter)

XOL DOG 400

thrill  **chill!**

BUNKER

10

On the corner of Albrechtstrasse, a bullet-pocked fortification looms over the frozen streets of Berlin. It's midnight, ten days before Christmas, 1996, and 400 hooded and booted gabbers are making a last stand. This WWII shelter has been their autonomous party space and second home for the last four years; now the *Polizei* are clearing them out, by force. Blaring threats over a PA system and armoured in riot gear, they're ready for violence. But these gabbers don't want a fight. They just want to share one more drilling-release under the blinking strobe at the Hard-Harder-Hardest Club on Earth.

"I arrived around 10 PM and everything was already a bit agitated," recalls Christian Müller, the EBM artist who forged his *radikale* terror-techno *Tanzmusik* as Xol Dog 400 within this concrete warren of cubicle dancefloors. Wearing dark shades and grey camo over faded black denim, he was the hero that night when he retaliated against the *Polizei*'s PA with sonic threats of his own, blaring from his car stereo. "People were dancing, the police were getting more angry," he continues. "Then they said, you have to shut down the music or we will seize your car. So I drove off."

Parked up outside another historic Berlin squat club, the ramshackle Eimer on Rosenthaler Strasse, the demo-party continued, foreshadowing a noisy counterattack that would take to the streets the following summer. This next parade would be a bit more organised, with trucks and people dancing in protest against the city that exiled them to the streets, and the techno family that had rejected them too.

Discovered by Tekknozid rave promoter and DJ Wolle XDP, who inaugurated the Hardest Club on Earth with a short run of Hartware parties, by '93 this 1,000-square-metre feat of Nazi engineering, sheering 18 metres into the sky, had been claimed by the Berliner terrorcore. These *Schmuddelkindern* preferred their techno harsh and punishing, pitched up to an unrelenting gallop, with all the Dutch gabber colour and silliness stripped away. Compared to Tresor, the Bunker was even more demanding and diehard than the city's original hardcore techno club. The Bunker was claustrophobic, frightening, airless, and fucking loud. The gabbers were relegated to the downstairs floor, sealed up in rooms, which kept changing every few months, to let the place air out. These walls, three metres thick, would be slick with sweat, and painted black to cover up the mould.

"The Bunker was probably the most reduced setup you can think of," says Christian. "It was taking the Tresor and making it even more extreme: so everything that was nice, you cut that off. No Globus bar, actually, no real bar at all. Just a dark room with concrete walls, and everything reduced to sound."

At the Bunker club, the Berlin gabber-terrorcore scene evolved in tolerance alongside the city's sex-positive techno culture incubating in other parts of the building, comprising 120 rooms split over five floors. Snax, the men-only leather and rubber fetish nights (or "Pervy Parties") from Norbert Thormann and Michael Teufele, moved into the Bunker from summer '94; paving the route to Berghain, which would open ten years later. Whilst sex-positive club Kit Kat grew from the Rot-Kreuz-Klub, housed in the medical barracks outside and connected by a courtyard, where all these communities freely mingled.

The Bunker was one of the last spaces in Berlin where the gabbers felt accepted amongst the rest of the city's outliers. "Gabber ended up at Bunker because there was no other place for it," confirms Tanith, who quit his Tresor residency to play with Wolle at the Bunker during the first Hartware parties. "Tresor wasn't interested in gabber," he adds. "Tresor was a different hard to Bunker. It was more Underground Resistance hard, not gabber hard."

"For our youth generation, to be cool you had to go at least one time to the Bunker and hear that freaking sound," says Beagle from Gabba Nation, the crew who inherited Friday nights at Bunker from Wolle from '93. Beagle was already making music with childhood friend Bullfrog, and together with Glurff they became the Gabba Nation live act, alongside the crew's founders and chief Bunker residents, DJ Cut-X and DJ Sascha.

"With Bullfrog we are playing with Playmobil at the birthdays of our parents, and ten years later we are playing with the computer and drum machines," says Beagle. "I've felt music since I can think."

Inspired by early Mono Tone records from The Speed Freak, the pair released their first records with Steffen Kuschel in Leipzig, minting one of the many hardcore labels within the Sound Base Music network. Except Beagle was mispronounced as Boogle on that first EP for War Records. He would end up managing the Gabba Nation label together with Sascha, and writing most of the crew's piercing, drill-down style of gabber-terror music, or "terrorcore" as it would be called.

For Beagle, there was no real musical distinction between the German gabba of Gabba Nation, and gabber from Holland. "For me music is music," he explains. "It doesn't depend on how you write it. It's slow, it's fast. It's everything, and it's written in many ways." The Berlin gabbers were defined more by their uncompromising, combative attitude. "In Berlin it was only hardcore, the rest is shit," Beagle explains. "I think hardcore people in Holland were much more open-minded. Berlin hardcore was like a little island at the end of the world."

"Bunker was my living room," says Christian Xol Dog. "I was there on

Sunday, climbing, talking to people. I was there every other night." His debut album, *Sons of T2*, captures the locked-in resonance of a New Years Eve party held inside one of the Bunker's many tomb-like dancefloors. Released via his EBM home label, KM-Musik, it came with the byline: "What hartcore really means and why one-hundred-fifty is slow." It was a bit too much for KM-Musik, says Christian, so he paid for the printing and pressing himself.

He explains the title is a homage to Tanith and Tresor's dungeon crucible beneath the Leipziger, where Christian experienced his first techno flash: "T2 was this notion from Tanith and Tillman. It was like an inside joke, TT for Tanith and Tillman, but also there was this fad to call hardcore with a 't' to make it even harder. I thought that I was actually the son of this or the offspring."

When Bunker closed down, the gabbers were forced into exile. The Eimer (named after the builder's bucket that hung outside the club as a secret beacon) became a temporary home. Originally squatted in 1990, this rundown house around the corner from the Bunker was "probably the most illegal club in Berlin," says Christian. "The floor between the ground floor and the cellar was broken down, so you could actually stamp on the first floor and look down to the people on the dancefloor." To reach the cellar dancefloor you could take the dodgy stairs, or slide down the old wheelbarrow chute. "It was really really dangerous," he adds, "so I was there a lot."

At the Eimer, anarcho punk and Spiral Tribe's nomadic-tekno bred with the terrorcore sound of the Bunker gabbers, and satellite scenes from Hamburg and Frankfurt. This Triangle of Core featured Hamburg's Nordcore GMBH collective, who gathered every Friday in the smoke-filled underground parking garage of the Box, until they were also kicked out by police in '96. Original PCP terrorists from FFM, featuring initiator Thorsten as Don Demon and Miro, the World's Hardest Kotzaak, played across the Box and the Bunker, alongside Frankfurt Bembel terror promoter and radio host Trauma XP. At the Eimer, lingering post-Reunification anxiety and gentrification fear mixed with anger against the *Polizei* across these outsider tribes, who all stood in solidarity together on July 12, 1997, for the first edition of the Hateparade.

It was christened Hateparade in opposition to love, because the Love Parade was its symbolic enemy: a carnival of commercialism, which in '96 had excluded these Berlin gabbers from joining. So they decided to have their own. "I was not really happy with that name," says Christian, part of the original group of organisers, led by Trauma XP. "I don't hate anybody." The following year it was renamed Fuckparade.

Aggression wasn't the goal, but animosity against the Love Parade was real. These gabbers had marched with the techno scene at the start of the decade, and now they were priced out from joining, and it hurt. "In the beginning the Love Parades were like a family gathering," explains Christian, "and the hardcore-gabber-terrorcore were part of the family."

"We played at the Love Parade in 1995 on the Mesh Truck," says Beagle, still a teenager at the time. "Then in '96 they didn't want hardcore on the Love Parade. So we did our thing."

Hateparade wasn't just marching against the "shit" music of the Love Parade, it was about raising the alarm to the hierarchies and the egos that had wormed into the heart of the movement. It was to be a warning – set to 200 BPM – as to where this commerce-led route might lead. "They were throwing cigarettes from cars and small bottles of Absolut Vodka and I thought, holy shit," says Christian. The Love Parade was Berlin's original street party-demo, born from hippy Reunification euphoria in the summer of '89. Five years later, one million techno revelers from around the world were massing beneath the golden Victory Column of the Strasse des 17. Juni, steered by a carefully curated selection of trucks and club partners.

"I always thought it was a great idea to do something against the Love

Parade," says Tanith, "even when I was part of the Love Parade." With his Stormtroopers of Peace throwing orange smoke bombs from a Soviet tank, Tanith caused provocation within the organisation over the early '90s editions. But even sympathetic Tanith, the Master of Nasty Sounds, thought the Fuckparade was too hostile: "For me the Fuckparade was always an anti thing," he explains. "It was like saying: you like it hard, no, but you get it if you want it or not. That's not for me."

For their anti-march, the gabbers inverted the Love Parade's logo, made from dots in a circular pattern increasing in size towards a central nested heart; turning the dots into hand grenades. On its inaugural run, three trucks, including a giant Russian Ural, loaned from a Friedrichshain squatter collective, led a procession of 1,000 terrorcore fans through the streets. Gabba Nation piled onto an open flatbed truck with a precarious stack of speakers and a whole table of gear, including two computer monitors, as their MC screamed "HAKKAHHHH!" to bystanders and overwhelmed police. There were no speeches, or much political motivation at all. That would come later. Most Hateparade attendees just wanted to dance, and make a statement on the streets.

"Of course, the police were alarmed and freaked out when I registered the demonstration," explains initiator Trauma XP in *The Definitive Oral History Of Berlin's Fuckparade*. "They really thought we wanted to smash up Berlin."

As the Hateparade gathered outside the police-sealed Bunker, on the other bank of the Spree, the Tiergarten was steadily turning into a latrine. As trash piled up beneath the crush of bodies during this record-breaking edition of the Love Parade, it was broadcast to the world as the grinning peak of the techno movement, with Berlin as its glorious and liberated capital. Imagine if these one million Love Parade dancers were all bald heads dressed in Australians, and chopping and flicking in the *hakke* dance?

"In the very early stages we had the ambition to go big," explains Irfan van Ewijk – the 'I' in ID&T – about the origins of Thunderdome, the rave that brought gabber to the masses. "Expedition halls instead of old warehouses. A nationwide movement. Not just the Amsterdam scene, we wanted to have everybody. Big, big, bigger!"

The first Thunderdome was held in an ice-skating arena in October 1992. It featured four relatively unknown DJs on the bill (who would go on to become superstars) and a colossal spinning fairground ride the team feared might crash through the ice rink floor. The promoters were two plucky twenty-year-old school friends from a village outside Amsterdam, still living at home. This was the second major event they had ever attempted, and 30,000 people turned up. "That first Thunderdome wasn't hardcore or gabber yet," says Duncan Stutterheim in *Release / Celebrate Life: The Story of ID&T*, chronicling the self-built company that would become one of the biggest success stories in Dutch Dance.

In 1992 Duncan Stutterheim, together with Irfan van Ewijk and Theo Lelie, founded ID&T, simultaneously launching the careers of individual DJs Dano, Gizmo, the Prophet and Buzz Fuzz as hardcore's first DJ super group, the Dreamteam. Within its first year Thunderdome had expanded into multiple events across the nation. ID&T invested in the Bad Vibes record store in Alkmaar, and a label, ID&T Music, to release the first Thunderdome compilation CD, featuring productions exclusively from the Dreamteam. It was the start of a commercial record empire that would ultimately fund Thunderdome (and ID&T) through its rapid expansion – and soundtrack a generation of youth worldwide.

"The CD sales saved our asses multiple times," van Ewijk admits. ID&T sold around 9,000 copies of that first Dreamteam CD; sales of later editions would exceed three million.

During the '94 gabber crisis, when the big hall gabber raves were limited or outright banned by local governments, Thunderdome went on a club tour, and pushed across its borders into Germany and Belgium, Spain and France. After making its debut at the Love Parade (the year the Berlin's Bunker gabbers were excluded), Thunderdome returned to Germany, bringing their big hall gabber rave to the SKH Sport & Kongresshalle in Schwerin, 100 KM outside of Hamburg. This time there was a second room, a strobing and confronting Terrordome, featuring acts from Germany's Triangle of Core: PCP's Don Demon and Stickhead, Christian Xol Dog 400 and Hamburg terrorists Nordcore performed their nosebleed-barrage of squat party breakneck beats in the foyer, as Thunderdome residents Waxweazle, Lady Dana and the Prophet played in the main hall.

Nordcore GMBH (acronym for Gabba Mutanten Bande Hamburg) had their own label, Nordcore Records, minted with the PCP-indebted 'Planet Hartcore' and the scuzzy 'Hartcore Will Never Die' on their four-track EP *Hartcore City Downtown*, released in '95. *Terrordome* was the name of their own Thunderdome-style compilation series, which they took over from Mokum, kicking out the Dutch gabber music to showcase Hamburg's homegrown terrorcore style to the world. Like the Berlin Bunker terrorcore sound, this was intensified gabber music, menacing and morose, made for open-ended partying in cramped dirty spaces, until the *Polizei* turn up.

The *Thunderdome* CDs, curated by Denis Doeland, AKA DJ Weirdo, doubled as advertising for upcoming Thunderdome events, releases and merch lines. They became iconic collectors' items to the Dutch gabbers massing at home – and abroad. Packaged in striking 80s airbrush cover designs by Victor Feenstra, featuring horror movie characters like Pennywise and Chucky, and other lurid-toned creatures of the night, the aesthetics were hard, scary and dark, but with a comic edge, like the music itself; appealing to rebellious school kids and hardcore diehards alike.

In '96 the Bunker gabbers released their own Thunderdome-Terrordome compilation, *Bunker Beats One*, with Christian Xol Dog managing the project. "The idea was to do what the Dutch did, but properly," he says about curating PCP nightmare terror by Miro as Jack Lucifer and heady experimental hardcore from Laurent Hô's label Epiteth Rec., who regularly played at the Box and the Bunker during this period. There was also plenty of minimal brutalism from Gabba Nation, like 'Hard? Mellow? Die!' from DJ Cut-X. It was a double CD release; the second featuring a track each from The Speed Freak and Laurent Hô was cut into the shape of a cassette tape. "The plan was to do more," adds Christian, "but the Bunker closed, the Pikosso label behind the release went bankrupt, and nobody would listen to Xol Dog about licensing a track anymore."

The Bunker label might have failed, but the Triangle of Core community kept growing, spreading into venues like the Stellwerk, and continuing to mass every July on the streets for Fuckparade. By 2000 this barbarous Love Parade counter demo was attracting 10,000 people to party all weekend to Praxis activist breakcore and Bunker-Hamburg-Frankfurt terror programmed over a series of events, bookending Saturday's main street procession. Christian recalls his experiences at the head of the demo: "I was pacing the parade, talking to the police, stopping sometimes," he explained. "I remember we were at some street slightly going uphill, and at the top of the hill I said okay, we stop now so that we can dance, and I look down the hill...Holy shit, there's 10,000 people!" He was unsure if they, as an organisation, had control of this anymore.

Even Love Parade attendees joined in "because they heard there's this cooler parade," says Christian. The Fuckparade was also considerably less crowded – as 1.3 million ravers crammed into Tiergarten. For Christian, it felt like the Fuckparade was becoming what they were marching against: "an underground interesting thing becoming a mainstream event," as he explains, "so we decided the 2001 Fuckparade would be the last."

In 2001, both parades lost their status as political demonstrations. It forced these rival organisations to politicise, or commercialise, which caused a schism in the largely apolitical Berlin gabber scene. "In the beginning it was cool to have the Fuckparade," Beagle explains, "I'm not a very political guy, and for me this Parade was about music, not politics. It drove the organisation into the left wing, and I didn't find this very honest."

Deliberately vague politics had enabled the Love Parade to attract sponsors and grow exponentially into one of Berlin's biggest global tourist attractions. When the organisation registered as a commercial street event in the spring of 2001, the city offered their financial support.

Fuckparade was going to end in 2001 anyways – but when they were told they couldn't march, now they had to. They were banned from having trucks and sound systems, so they planned a silent demo for that summer, with music played from portable radios tuned into Radio Fritz, who were set up in the foyer at the Volksbühne, where the Fuckaparde was due to end. Except the police were waiting for them at Frankfurter Tor, and confiscated all the radios. Organisers Trauma XP, Wolle XDP and Christian Xol Dog delivered a series of forced, impromptu speeches in front of the Volksbühne – Christian playing a sampled speech, in typical industrial-punk retaliation. Afterwards, a secret sound system from a VW bus kicked in, to quell the tension, as the first of many lawsuits were drafted by the Fuckparade against the city. Follow-up demos would become increasingly politicised, causing the alienated apolitical gabbers to take the party off the streets, and back into the clubs.

Five metres beneath the bustling Leipziger Strasse, enclosed within Tresor's bunker basement, the city's terrorcore reformed. Fridays at Tresor were renamed Tresor.core with weekly hardcore techno and speedcore nights programmed by local crews, including Gabba Nation presenting their new series, Speed Limit, on the first Friday of the month. On January 3, 2003, the Triangle of Core celebrated ten years of strobing sonic annihilation down here with Gabba Nation and Nordcore inviting NYC gabber-punks Lenny Dee and Rob Gee from Industrial Strength; with

Miro and FFM techno taking over Globus.

"It felt like hardcore was living again in Berlin," says Beagle, "like a new beginning." But the revival didn't last long. After years of circulating rumours of Tresor's impending closure, it finally happened in 2005, after this prime plot of real estate was finally sold off for office spaces.

The world's first hardcore techno club celebrated fourteen years of dancing into oblivion with the closing party to end all closing parties, which lasted for more than two weeks. "I can't remember how we survived this," says Carola Stoiber. The Tresor Records manager turned forty over this bittersweet fortnight, where the greatest names in house and techno from around the world came to mourn and celebrate the site where techno culture rose from the rubble to engulf the world.

Crowds lined the Leipziger for days, clamouring to get in, as bodies sought respite from its demanding dancefloor in the heaving garden outside, where the message loomed definitely from above: It's not Over. A promise the Tresor team were determined to keep. This was also the title of the accompanying techno compilation. The event itself was called The Final Cut, in a nod to the label's foundations, with Chris Liebing and original resident Tanith playing the first night, on April 1, with Richie Hawtin and Ricardo Villalobos headlining the official close.

In True Tresor Spirit, the basement Sunday finale was handed over to its Wednesday night family: local residents Kriek, Dash, Mack, DJ Dry, Baeks and Pacou, had built their loyalist midweek community playing behind Tresor's iconic prison bars as part of DJ Niplz's young talent series, Headquarters, inaugurated the decade before. It was morning on April 19, when time was called on the longest-running techno party in history, and the heavy steel doors of this forgotten bank vault were finally closed. In the crisp Spring dawn, the last of the Tresor diehards, faces streaked with tears and sweat, huddled together in groups of nameless eternal friendship, shared the last smoke before asking one another: so where to next?

A period of "exile" followed as Tresor's team searched for a new location, eventually scoring keys to the Kraftwerk power station on Köpenicker Strasse — the same street as the original UFO club. After a difficult period of renovations and issues with the authorities, which saw co-founder Dimitri Hegemann enlist Tibetan monks to "cleanse" the space with a week-long ritual, Tresor finally reopened on May 24, 2007, with Frankfurt's Sven Väth topping the bill. But the comeback wasn't easy. "In the two years without Tresor, there was a lot happening, also in Berlin," says Carola, "the scene was changing, and changing radically."

When Tresor closed in 2005, Berlin's terrorcore struggled to find a new base. "We always had problems trying to get venues," says Beagle. "We were the dirty freaks of Berlin techno." Even the Eimer squatters were finally evicted from their ramshackle house on Rosenthaler Strasse in 2003, ending one of the longest-enduring illegal clubs in Berlin. And when Tresor reopened, the gabbers were not welcome back. "If the momentum had continued then we would be in a different place now," Beagle concludes. "It was like a runaway train, but then everything went down again."

The punks, the squatters and the rest of the *Schmuddelkindern* were cast back out onto Berlin's traffic-clogged streets, now lined with commercial offices and shops, instead of the ruinous autonomous free party zones of the past. Fuckparade had no choice but to continue marching, in obstinate protest, in defiance, because fuck it we can!

ALLE IM EIMER!
Abflug: 22 Uhr
1999
Sonntag
11 JULI
LOVE & FUCK CHILL-OUT
LIVE
XOL DOG 400
DJS
DJ LAURENT HO
·TECHNO AUS FRANKREICH·
DJ SPEICHE
DJ TRAUMA XP
DJ Schwarzfahrer
·PLUS DJs/Acts·
CUT-X
BEAGLE
LONELY FREAK
V8
Video Installation
F. P. F. RAMPAZZO
Im Eimer
rosent
ler str. 68, berlin-mitte

HARTCORE WILL NEVER DIE!

31/12

NORDCORE-GMBH
BSE-DJ-TEAM
NORDCORE-PSYCHOPATH
AND A LOT OF FRIENDS

nordcore records
THE BOX HH
Price 15,- DM

BOX
Watch out for
NORDCORE RECORDS
1st Release 01/96
NC.R.666

IT'S
TRESOR

TRESOR
IT'S NOT OVER
LEAVING HOME / 01-16. APRIL 2005
Kasse
Kasse

THE FINAL THUNDERCLAP

11

By the end of the '90s Holland's one million gabbers, who once walked the streets with gabber pride, their own names stitched into the backs of their bomber jackets, had become a national joke. "People started to associate you with the parodies they saw on the television," explains Bobby Jacques, a gabber-turned-collector from Rotterdam, in the documentary *Uniform*. "The whole culture became a caricature. When I look back from my own perspective, I can remember that being a gabber meant something, you had a certain status. But that all changed."

With artists and fans alike choosing to grow out their hair and pack up their beloved Australian-brand tracksuits, a new sound and youth culture emerged in reaction against the decade of gabber stigmas. Hooliganism, racially motivated violence, drugs, negative media profiling, commercial exploitation, ridicule, parodies and extended overexposure on a massive scale all contributed to the next gabber crisis that the Dutch scene wasn't so quick to recover from.

"The hardcore scene had really collapsed, it was a mess," says Thunderdome co-founder Irfan van Ewijk in *Release / Celebrate Life: The Story of ID&T.*

For the first year since its inception, the 2000 edition of Thunderdome didn't happen. It was due to take place in Ghent, but influential neighbours complained, and ID&T had to cancel. ID&T Music, the recording empire that funded the raves, was also suffering from dwindling CD sales and a rapidly deteriorating relationship with its major label partner, Arcade, who had been sold off to Dutch newspaper publishers Wegener during the hardcore boom in '97. *Thunder Mag*, previously the most popular music magazine in the Netherlands with a peak circulation of 35,000, was also finished, and the Thunderdome website was taken offline. The brand that had turned Holland's hyper-local scenes into a nationwide movement, and global export, seemed to have crumbled under its own success.

Thunderdome was only put on hold for a while – it returned in 2001 – but something irreversible happened during the blackout: ID&T lost its heart for hardcore. From 2000 onwards founders Duncan Stutterheim, Irfan van Ewijk and their team began investing heavily in trance. Sensation and Tiësto became ID&T's new flagships as Holland's big hall gabber rave musically reinvented itself through the millennium.

For the first four years of the 2000s, Thunderdome was pushed in a new industrial direction by Sebastian Hoff, AKA Promo. As hardcore went pop in the latter half of the '90s, Hoff went back to hardcore's dark, raw genesis, to the hardcore techno of the Mover and PCP. Hoff's hardcore was much slower, darker and moodier, captured on his seminal series of EPs, *The Promo Files*, released through ID&T Music between '98 and '99.

After the Promo Files, Hoff was brought on to manage Thunderdome parties and CD series with Martijn Mobron (DJ X-Ess), who was working at ID&T Music in A&R. Their first party together, at the Heineken Music Hall in Amsterdam, featured acts like Manu Le Malin, Simon Underground and The DJ Producer. "We just totally changed it," says Hoff. "We kicked out all the mainstream stuff to try and reinvent the look and direction of Thunderdome." It wasn't well attended, but it did set a precedent for a more adventurous phase in Thunderdome's bookings.

By the mid-'00s, hardcore had shattered into several subgenres. "What I wanted to do was put them all back together again, in one room," explains

Andre van Zuijlen AKA MC Justice about his first Thunderdome program (with Gerard Zwijnenburg) at the Jaarbeurs from 2006. Like Hoff, he put together a challenging lineup for his first edition, giving peak-time slots to (then) relatively new names and mixing up the subgenres. For the terror MC – who performed at the Fuckparade, not the Love Parade – Thunderdome served as the ideal platform for introducing hardcore fans to different styles, "because, in my opinion it's all hardcore," he says.

In 2010, he enacted his dream at Thunderdome's Breaking Barriers event at the Jaarbeurs. Instead of multiple genre-based dancefloors, one big hall was set up with a stage in the centre, divided into four "rooms" by soundproof curtains. The subgenres included dubstep and crossbreed (a mix of hardcore and drum 'n' bass "invented" by the Outside Agency). Other "rooms" featured the fast and bouncy Frenchcore (no longer the industrial, cold, abstract sound of Parisian warehouses in the '90s) and more popular mainstream and early hardcore styles. Everyone was kept separate until 1 AM, when an alarm went off and the curtains were raised to reveal the centre stage, and the party symbolically united.

Justice also ran Thunderdome Radio from 2006 to 2013, along with one of Thunderdome's earliest and most iconic MCs, Da Mouth Of Madness. Starting out with DJ Uzi as the original "dynamic duo," running in the hip hop crew II Damn Dope from the late '80s, Uzi and Sietse Mouth Of Madness played their first Thunderdome gig together in 1995 as part of the Thunderdome XI On Tour, quickly turning into another of Thunderdome's flagship acts.

From the tour, Sietse became host of *TMF Hakkeeh*, an *MTV*-styled lifestyle show for gabbers, broadcast on Monday nights. "I hated *TMF*," Sietse admits. "I hated the way they portrayed gabbers and how they commercialised the lifestyle I loved so much." Unlike the show's other host, the parody act Gabber Piet, Sietse (later with Drokz by his side) brought the true hardcore to *TMF*, showcasing the diehard devotion of fans and artists via a segment called *De Gabber Kruk*, interviewing gabbers whilst sitting on a barstool in the middle of ID&T raves. When *TMF Hakkeeh* ended, Sietse remained in broadcasting, hosting Thunderdome Radio with DJ Promo, Catscan and DJ X-Ess between 2003 and 2005, when it was a weekly show on ID&T Radio, and then as co-anchor with Justice from 2006.

This second iteration of Thunderdome Radio was streamed live every Wednesday night, from 8 PM until midnight, from Studio 80 to over 30,000 listeners worldwide. It became renowned as much for breaking new talents as for its pranks. Thunderdome Radio's final transmission took place on December 18, 2013, at the BEAT Club in Amsterdam, in front of 600 people – one year after Thunderdome held its final rave at the RAI.

ID&T's last Thunderdome was named The Final Exam, after the party that launched this daredevil dance music company two decades earlier. All the crucial Thunderdome acts, past and present, reunited for one final blowout. It even brought the first Lady of hard dance, Dana van Dreven, back into the spotlight. Next to the Dreamteam, Dana racked up the most Thunderdome appearances during her residency. Dressed always in black when she plays, a real vinyl collector and B-side lover, the typically tall, blond and smiling Thundergod remains a role model for women in the harder styles, playing hardcore as Lady Dana and hardstyle as Dana. Through the scene's millennial rebrand, she became one of Holland's top-ranking DJs, until a burnout and series of health issues forced her to retire.

Dana started spinning vinyl as a teenager and for a long time was the only woman DJ in the Dutch scene, playing her first ID&T gig at Mysteryland for the Thunderdome stage. For twelve years she was a fixture at the Dutch festival, performing an unbelievable six times at her last Mysteryland, in 2008. She had to stop because it had become physically painful for her to continue playing records – but she wasn't going to miss the final Thunderdome.

"I was wearing a sling," she recalls. "I had one arm, so I played with my good friend Peter, DJ Uzi." Uzi and Dana weren't musically an ideal match, but they made it work. "To look into the crowd and have everybody smiling to see me, that made it all worthwhile," she says. "I was really confused about my future at the time and ended up loving the event so much that it gave me energy to keep fighting."

The decision to stop Thunderdome in 2012 didn't come easily. Throughout the '90s, Thunderdome was the leading hardcore brand. But during hardcore's second evolution, it was supplanted by other more contemporary brands, like Bass D and King Matthew's Masters Of Hardcore and Jan Lok's B2S in Rotterdam. Huge hardcore meetups, which Thunderdome pioneered, became more commonplace and as Dutch hardcore rapidly professionalised from a scene to an industry.

This chimed with the rise of EDM in the US, where Duncan Stutterheim had relocated with his family, and where ID&T had set their sights. Like lots of people at the time, they wanted a "piece of the EDM pie," as Gert van Veen writes in *The Story of ID&T*. They had entered into talks with Pasquale Rotella from Insomniac Events (Electric Daisy Carnival) and SFX Entertainment's Robert Sillerman about strengthening their position in the US, and hardcore didn't really fit with ID&T's new EDM vision. The official announcement that Thunderdome 2012 would be its last was made during Dominator Festival in July, just five months before the final event at the RAI. The following year, SFX Entertainment acquired 100% of ID&T.

The Final Exam marked the end of an era. But there was one person at the company who refused to let Thunderdome – or his gabber culture – die. Francois Maas, AKA The Field Marshall, had joined ID&T in 1999 as part of the promotions team and is one of the company's longest-serving employees. He's the reason Thunderdome still exists. "It's the brand I grew up with, and my best friend," he says. From 2013, Maas took it upon himself to "protect" the Thunderdome brand, in secret, until its inevitable return, organising pop-up events and Thunderdome Die Hard fan days, and new lines of merch and compilation CDs – all without ID&T knowing.

As the gabber movement rebranded into hardcore in the convention centres and big halls of Holland, the diehard gabber scene retreated back into the crucible clubs and youth centres, to rebuild in the shadows. This scene has remained separate and distinct from the Dutch megaraves, as well as its myriad hardcore subgenres and tribes.

"Hardcore is for everyone, gabber is not," explains neo-gabber Daniel Rønhave AKA Peckerhead from Copenhagen. Born in the '90s the self-described "outsider" has been flying the flag for contemporary gabber at home since 2010, and in the Netherlands as a mainstay of Mokum since 2017. "Gabber for me is the unity and friendship of all the people I've met in this subculture," he continues. "It's people I trust in good times and bad times, in crazy situations and steady ones. It's the ultimate connection you can have, where there's no borders, no countries, no limits."

In his productions, Pecky mines the past with passion and sensitivity, adding his own "Danish trancy" signature to records that convey the old school gabber spirit, brought chopping into the present. Whilst there are some introspective moments on his 2023 debut album for Mokum, *Dreams & Doubts* – in reference to feeling like a "tourist" in the Dutch gabber scene – this music comes alive on the dancefloor. 'I'm Being Repressed' is one of his faster "terrorist-style" album tracks, which he describes as "like screaming under water", whilst 'Compassion' with the lyric "we all exploit each other to survive" is about "being fucking young and reckless". These tracks also reveal a sense of urgency and frustration, from an outsider-artist fighting through an industry with more than just musical barriers.

When Pecky DJs, he only ever plays his own music, or music from friends. "That's my agenda," he says, "I like my own weird Danish Style. I really feel it and I want the audience to feel that I'm having a good time while I'm playing."

His first encounter with gabber culture happened in Rotterdam in 2008. He was barely eighteen on a fourteen-hour bus ride full of strangers, heading to A Nightmare – Paul Elstak's original Energiehal rave – at the Ahoy convention centre. "I was skint, I was scared, and I didn't fit in," he recalls. "When I finally got home after this two-day bender, I swore I was never going to go back to Holland again, and this music I would have nothing more to do with it." He pauses, a charismatic storyteller. "One month later, I find myself in the Netherlands again." Eventually, he moved to Rotterdam to fulfil the Dreams part of his album, but the Doubts kept getting in the way.

Peckerhead started as a street art project, by a DIY graphic designer wanting to make his mark on the world. "I just took a selfie of myself, cut off half the head because I saw Ruffneck do that," he explains about plastering his face up around town before Peckerhead became an outlet for his music. "It became like a schizophrenic project about how I wanted to be in a society that doesn't really exist," he elaborates. "I grew up in a place where people would yell at you on the street and say 'walk on the sidewalk, it's not a playground!'. Then I would be the only one walking around, bald head with a bomber jacket, being the weird guy."

It wasn't until he discovered hardcore in Holland that he finally felt welcome – "as long as you're humble and genuine," he adds.

This is the vibe of Københardcore, his intimate family-run party series, which he co-founded in 2017 with friend Klaus Boss, whose living room is wall to wall with vinyls. Pecky's younger "twin" brother is the Københardcore logo. "We have tons of banners with his face now at the party and this is so weird, but good, you know. It's his project too," he explains. The Peckerhead tagline – "not a normal day since 1992" – is also a tribute to his brother, born in '92. "And that's really what it's about," he notes. "It's just Brotherly Love, I want him to be a part of it, and a part of me, until we die."

Pecky has become integrated into the Dutch gabber-rave continuum, which has since turned into a proud street subculture once more. Gen Z gabbers don these '90s relics, which has encouraged some of the old guard gabbers to dust off theirs too, whilst early brands like Amsterdam-based Cyndium and their Pandemonium rave continue to pack out the gabber temples. The media picketing has ended, but the diehard Jesus Bus Evangelists are still around, handing out their lollipops and flyers.

Pandemonium celebrated twenty years on November 16, 2024, with a historic meeting in the gabber-gym temple of the Sporthallen Zuid. Pecky had the honour of presenting the peaktime Megamix, sharing the mainstage with the God of the Godfathers, Marc Acardipane, and personal heroes, like Ruffneck. Just before his set, he was sitting beneath the scaffolding propping up the stage, noise-cancelling headphones pumping soothing music through his racing mind.

Performing beneath a projection-mapped troll, artfully crude and technological at the same time, Pecky delivered a maelstrom of silly voices and neurotic psycore, whipped up with rave stabs and vintage hoover sounds, to a glistening gabber soup of old and new ravers bashing out their fears and doubts and rage until there was nothing left, no thoughts at all. When the lights came on a few hours later, silence filled the Sporthallen Zuid as these satiated gabbers shuffled quietly off into the night, ready to face the week.

KØBENHARDCORE

CLIQUE

CGN
Camp Go' Na

NEO-RAVE ARMAGEDDON

12

It's an unusually sunny Sunday for the North of England, and Pontins Southport Holiday Park is eerily calm. There are a few stragglers from last night splashing in the pond that's not really a pond in the centre of this 70s seaside detention camp. There's a bit more action by the trampolines, and a queue has formed for the go-karts. Health and Safety can fuck off, indeed.

Outside the Queen Vic pub, the smoking area is thick with day drinkers and people still awake from Thursday. Inside the pub, the sticky dancefloor ebbs with ravers in various states of cohesion to all the rave music you don't get to hear anywhere else, all at once, in fancy dress. Rarely does it dip below the upper-most echelons of beats per minute, and everyone wears a Cheshire Cat grin. There's not a sad soul in the place. Even the Superhero who's slumped over himself in a corner is smiling from ear to ear, whilst the bar staff in oversized four-leaf-clover hats cheerily serve the constant stream of totally mental nut nut let's go ardkore British punters, plus Belgians, Dutch, and the rest of the worldwide Hard Crew.

In the Bang Room (or is it the Face Room?) improv jazz musician and DIY software maker Squarepusher presents his latest reinvention of the broken beat medium, the techy glitch sounds of *Damogen Furies*, which he plays behind a fencing mask – turning himself into the visuals that slash across the screen set up behind. It's high-tech and uber nerdy, but also made for raving.

This Weekender is about the music, and getting on it, in equal measure. It's Full-on Mask Hysteria, Scottish Rezerection resurrected, and Roland puns reign supreme.

The holiday camp setting "allows people to put more effort in," founder James Gurney explained to *The Guardian*. "You've got a base where you can keep costumes; it's a sanctuary that you can go to. And everyone's having a little house party." Some people go just for the chalet parties, but then they're missing out on the singular "neo-rave explosion" of dance music styles that Bang Face delivers every time, in a three-day, three-room mashup, best experienced by getting fully stuck in.

Squarepusher headlined the inaugural Weekender in Camber Sands from 2008, and has remained on heavy rotation ever since (alongside brother Ceephax Acid). Back then, the second room hosted a Detroit electro takeover, with Juan Atkins and "Mad" Mike Banks playing Model 500's first-ever live UK show, alongside Dopplereffekt and Drexian affiliate DJ Stingray. Dub legend Aba Shanti-I was also there. Plus Chas & Dave, the "rabbit, rabbit, rabbit" pub-pop duo. There was a pool party with MC Sharkey, DJ Squid Vicious and DJ Ozzy Frogspawn, and an opening ceremony hosted by Normski, former anchorman of the '90s TV program *Dance Energy* – the *BBC*'s raving alternative to *Top of the Pops*.

These kaleidoscopic raving Weekenders have taken place annually in the UK ever since, except for 2013, when it was cancelled because of complaining neighbours, and in 2014, when Bang Face went to Belgium and Holland instead. But the Weekenders are only one part of a long and looping story that begins much, much earlier, in an old public toilet in Shoreditch.

The first Bang Face party took place on October 17, 2003, and was christened The Birth of Neo-Rave. "Neo-rave was just some nonsense I made up," says Gurney, characteristically dismissive. "But it represented a need to re-inject fun and raving back into parties, which had become pretty serious – especially in London at the time."

Every Bang Face has been lovingly documented in the Bang Face archives, evidence that, despite the seeming uncouthness, there was a plan and a vision from the start, which began like a raucous house party. The first few were free, and word quickly spread that they were, at their core, a bit of a laugh.

"I wasn't having much fun after leaving art college so decided to start DJing again," continues Gurney, who always closes the Weekenders, playing in a red cape lined with glow sticks, as Saint Acid. "I used to play acid sets years before – hence the name – but this time I felt like playing all the banging tracks I had," says Saint Acid from St Albans, with long auburn hair.

The neo-rave of Bang Face implied rave for the next generation, where parties were volatile, eclectic and predictable in their unpredictability. You knew what you were going to get from a Bang Face event, without knowing exactly what. During its literal underground days, banging out the bangers beneath the dirty paving slabs of London, Bang Face went through a few small venue changes. Within the cramped sardine can of Trafik, the Hard Crew concept was born: the name for the Bang Face community, which extends to punters and artists alike, because everyone who goes to Bang Face is honorary Hard Crew. It's a riff on the members-only rave clubs of the '90s, like Sterns in Worthing and its infamous basement "kickdrum pit".

"It felt more like a social club," says Gurney. "So I get why people loved those days. There certainly was a special connection between everyone there and the music." He fondly recalls live acid sets from Ceephax Acid Crew and Mike Dred "on tables with everyone crowded round" as some of his favourite memories from this period.

"You go to a lot of parties and there's a bit of danger there, like, you're not quite sure whether there's going to be violence or not," says Planet Mu's Paradinas, who who ran his own Ammunition events during this period at the Electrowerkz, the North London warehouse venue where outlier club tribes from Slimelight to fetish club Torture Garden have thrived since the '80s. Ammunition brought the Planet Mu continuum sound to the Electrowerkz, as the introverted trainer-gazing weed haze of dubstep and berating MC boys club of grime took over London. Bang Face added inflatable balloons and rave horns to the mix. "It was a nice relief to go to a party where everyone dresses up, and it's a bit like a kid's birthday party," adds Mike, who ended his Ammunition run as Bang Face moved in.

Lineup-wise, Bang Face and Ammunition tapped the same musical vein, and Planet Mu has always featured heavily at the Bang Face; but they did not share the same vibe. "Bang Face was unashamedly retro," says Mike, "and all the better for it."

Where Ammunition looked to the future – backing the edgier dubstep sound of Vex'd and Manucian rappers Virus Syndicate – Bang Face kept a line open for the Helter Skelter madheads, and nerdier weirdos, like Rephlex (Mike's first home label when he made his giggly (un)intelligent dance music debut in the '90s). As the UK rave continuum shifted gears through the millennium, and popular nights fell out of fashion, Bang Face thrived, sounding a rave horn for all the oddball genres that were never popular or cool.

On September 9, 2005, Bang Face joined the Electrowerkz family with its 303 Musketeers theme event (named "in honour of Cardinal Richelieu's birthday in 1585," allegedly). It had a distinct acid theme, with A Guy Called Gerald, Baby Ford and Luke Vibert all billed. Every Bang Face is named according to the date of the party, from the Electrowerkz meet on October 14, 2005, honouring the 1066 Battle of Hastings – or rather 10606 featuring Kid 606 playing; to 2016's Bangy McBang Face edition of the Bang Face river boat rave across the Thames. "Come dressed as Ravid Attenborough explorers and endangered species," prompted the flyer. On July 20, 2007, Bang Face paid raving tribute to the Riot Act during one of its three takeovers at Glade festival, featuring two rave veterans, Vibert and the Ragga Twins, making a nostalgic comeback.

"James came to me with all these white labels of instrumentals they never released," Vibert explains about teaming up with the Shut Up And Dance Spliffheads. "So the first time I played with them it was completely their music. They were so chuffed," says Vibert. "You can tell they haven't done it for years." Vibert is one of the many Bang Face residents who plays whenever the call comes in: "I'm always happy to fill in," he says about stepping up whenever an act goes awry. "The first couple I was playing every day."

"Promoters have this dream of creating the perfect rave," says Ned Beckett from Little Big, who first invited Bang Face for a takeover at Glade Festival. "Bang Face was a very specific, very special scenario. They needed full control of the production, the venue and everything to be able to do what they do." The Glade takeovers primed the way to the Weekenders, and the hundreds of inflatables, tens of thousands of glow sticks, and motivational signage that came with it. "Not often you can say you DJed in a snowstorm of inflatable beach balls," says Luke DJ Producer. "It really is as mental as possible."

Luke has been hardcore raving and a hardcore rave DJ since the acid house free party days, aligning with the Universe rave crew in Somerset, and playing techno to the breakbeat crowd since late '92. Formally playing hip hop under the name DJ Quickcut, he earned his "producer" moniker not because he was making music: "I didn't even know what production was," he explains. "I said to my friend, why this name? He said, 'dude: because you produce the goods'. And it stuck, and that was it."

He (fatally, or fatefully) connected with Hellfish at the Helter Skelter Technodrome one night in 1996. Fish was waving a white label in his face with a weird look in his eye. "Then I put this record on: a white label of Deathchant 04 [by Diplomat]," says Luke, "and that was the beginning of a really long and beautiful and turgid relationship." He laughs; frenemies to the end.

Turntablist and troller Hellfish recounts his side of the meeting: "Contrary to public belief, the first time I met Producer was on West-on-super-Mare beach. I was on holiday in 1995 with my uncle Frank (RIP). Luke and his mate Simon Scorpio were taking part in a sponsored world record sandcastle building attempt. As I recall, I was just chilling on the beach with Frank drinking beers when this b-boy ice-cream van pulled up emitting 'Ice ice baby' from its tannoy, Lukad Producer jumped out the back with a spade and a massive boombox. A few beers later, and I can't remember exactly what happened, just that after their disastrous record attempt we got chatting and it turned out that they were playing b2b that night in Bristol. We ended up swapping a promo copy of Deathchant 02 for four 99 flakes and a couple of cider lollies."

Producer and Hellfish have been raining breakbeats and gabber kicks down on Bang Face since the Weekenders began, and no Bang Face sesh is complete without a Deathchant moshpit. They've been keeping the Loftgroover tradition alive (who played a drum 'n' bass set at the 2022 Weekender).

Luke recalls their flaming back to back set at the Trevelgue Holiday Park in Newquay for the historic Cornish Weekender – the edition Aphex Twin headlined. "About twenty minutes into the set, I was looking across the auditorium and I could count about four separate mosh pits," says Luke. "I was like, 'Fish, are you getting this?' It was the most outrageous violent disgusting outburst of rave-idiocy I've ever seen in my life. It was like a flashpoint. After that, Bang Face, every time: next level."

British humour and breakbeats (almost always combined in the British breakcore scene) have been the core of Bang Face hardcore. "The first time Shitmat played it was a very significant moment," says Gurney. "The energy and humour were spot on." When the Weekenders began, Shitmat's performance art-party and netlabel crew Wrong Music were assigned to the Bang Face TV station. Streaming total nonsense to every chalet on site, the first BFTV shows featured homemade cartoons about blue shapes living in Skol cans who went on strange adventures, as well as "adverts" and interviews. There were films too, to while away the time between raves, like Dave Skywalker's BFTV premier of *The Story of Y*, as well as the chance for anyone at Bang Face to come down and perform.

Then came the Wrong Music takeovers, or Wrong Disco, as they were called. Past editions have included a full outing of the Countryside Alliance Crew performing "rural" remakes of pop and dance tunes, and *Trong The Musical*, a Wrong Music rendition of Tron. "Trying to do a modern, video-based overture theatre piece at a rave is the best way to explain it," says Shitmat.

There's never a dull moment at Bang Face. This isn't passive festival consumerism, you're involved and engaged from the unpredictable opening ceremony – including record-breaking glow sticks, mock beheadings and flying – to deplorable close. Pull the rip chord, and here's your emergency escape slide from the plunging crises of 21st century life. It has also resurrected a few rave career-casualties along the way.

Altern 8's Mark Archer credits the support of Gurney and Bang Face as being key to the continuation of his career – which took a dive after things went sour between him and his music partner Chris Peat. "I lost that many gigs, I lost my house and all the rest of it because it got that bad," he says. "But James stood by me all the way."

Altern 8 wrote themselves into the ledgers of dance music history over the first half of the '90s. Together with dancer Martyn Cresswell, a robot on stilts, tanks, pranks and other paraphernalia, Altern 8 were Bang Face before Bang Face. The antithesis of Archer and Peat's first Detroit techno project, Nexus 21, Altern 8 didn't take themselves seriously, and the British public loved it. Altern 8's 1992 debut album *Full-On Mask Hysteria* epitomised a unique and fleeting period in Britain, which still lives on the Bang Face dancefloor.

"They aren't in it for any commercial or financial reasons," says Beckett, whilst managing to endure over two decades and against multiple odds. "They're in it because they have this vision, this perfect rave moment," which has retained the intimate members-only vibe of their first free events, now with 5,000 Hard Crew. "It's really important for me to keep the values the same," says Gurney. "We've stayed true to the original spirit that the party always comes first."

Just as it feels like the raving euphoria is about to wane, a white placard pops up with a message perfectly suited for the moment. "The text banners developed around the idea of having motivational phrases on the dancefloor," says Gurney. "Like the ravers being the MCs but without a mic." They mostly included obnoxious catchphrases like "piss me quick," and "the only thing I am fucking tonight are my prospects," plus all the Roland puns imaginable: "pieces of 808," "page 303 girls" and "909 red balloons," to name a few.

Bang Face lit a glow stick trail to the 2010s with its IRL meme-party culture and silly programming done with the utmost seriousness, whilst its neo-rave soundtrack has been adopted by the raving masses of the 2020s. But Bang Face wouldn't be Bang Face without the Hard Crew, the hardcore of the hardcore, getting safely mangled up together in this giant rubber dinghy scudding across the rest of the world.

PHUTURE GABBERS

13

On hardcore's jubilee year, the Dutch rave that brought gabber to the masses returned. 40,000 fans from around the world descended upon the Jaarbeurs convention centre in Utrecht on October 28, 2017, for the biggest Thunderdome ever, with more than 80 artists and MCs reuniting under the balled up fists of the Thunderdome's iconic Wizard.

At the Thundergods stage an older crowd revelled in their former rebel youth, singing along to cult classics like Speedy J's epochal Rotterdam anthem (and Feyenoord football chant) 'Pullover', played from a DJ booth enshrined in a wall of TVs flashing colourful graphics. With its low ceiling and party vibe unlike anywhere else in the building, this was the original community having their own Thunderdome within the megarave's maze of turnstiles and Australian tracksuits, as 20,000 people gathered in the main arena for DJ Promo's special twenty-five years of hardcore set.

The set ends with 'Locker Room Talk' by the Outside Agency, written around a sample from Donald Trump's controversial *Access Hollywood* tape (among other things). When the sample drops, the American president's face appears on the giant LED screen behind the DJ booth as he is branded a "pussy grabber". It's barbarous, satirical and totally hardcore, as brutal as it is hilarious. At the start of the set, dancers in white chemical suits and gas masks stormed the stage with flares during the Dance Ecstasy 2001 classic 'Slaves To The Rave', written by Marc Acardipane.

The God of the Godfathers plays beneath an enormous clown with bulging eyes and a flame of hair at the Heroes arena, raising up his drum machine sampler like a guitar, beneath the Pennywise character's bared teeth (and cover of *Thunderdome VIII – The Devil In Disguise*). As an artist obsessed with the year 2017, since the very first 1990 PCP white label, his comeback seemed inevitable – or was it fate?

In 2017 he officially resurrected his most personal and underrated alias, the Mover, to perform at techno festivals all over Europe. Unlike his other 80 or so aliases, which were dreamt up characters with ludicrous backstories, the Mover is a real nickname. "This is 100% me," he says. "I'm born in April, Aries, which means that 'doesn't work' doesn't exist for me. There's always a way. I always find a solution. I'm the solution man, that's why I move things."

From the embers of his own doom prophecy, Marc was compelled to write *Undetected Act From The Gloom Chamber*, the first new Mover album since 2002's *Frontal Frustration* for Tresor. *Gloom Chamber* is ominous but not as oppressive as you might expect. It's the burnt-out embodiment of rave, pierced through with Mentasm jabs, which decades later have become weapons of nostalgia, sounding out past traumas rather than phuture ones. As ever, it's the wrenchingly morose melodies that has this record functioning at some deeper level, but it was more difficult to finish than the hundreds Marc has dashed off in the past.

"It's harder to finish and record tracks as I get older because I'm more of a perfectionist; when you're younger you don't give a fuck about these things," he told *Juno*.

The record was ready for release at the end of 2017, and was even debuted live in Berlin alongside sets from The Horrorist, Neil Landstrumm and PCP mainstay Miro. "Nothing I played there made it onto the album," he says. "I had polished it until it was so complex I thought I could never perform it live, and it's not this raw Mover sound anymore." Apart from one track, the entire record was scrapped and rewritten in the intuitive and speedy fashion of his youth; *Gloom Chamber* is this second, more stripped-back iteration.

Marc has always written music quickly, so long as "the feeling is right in the beginning." *The Final Sickness* took a single day to complete – "production, writing, mixing, everything." 'I Like It Loud' was finished in a few hours. 'Stereo Murder,' minutes. This rapid production process partly explains his prolific output and former need for so many aliases, which became more complicated to manage in the era of social media.

Gloom Chamber may have been rewritten in a blinding atomic flash, but his Mover music comes from years of smouldering speculation. Over the decades, the alias served as a conduit for post-Cold War fears morphing into millennial terror. Mover music, he claims, is a form of sonic therapy, where tracks are "painkillers" and the act of writing music is like "self-medicating," offering rosy respite for those willing to marinate its black and blue beauty. "The Mover is depressive but always with hope," he says. "There is dark negative and dark positive, and the Mover is dark positive."

Before disbanding in '97, the original message of PCP was to teach people the hard feeling, conjured by a drum machine pulse rattling through a corrugated iron roof and the guttural reverb of a few MCs shining a flashlight to a waking nightmare, more terrifying than any Freddy Kruger or Pinhead, because this shit was real.

"This was such a special moment," says Marc of the group's last live show together, performing to 10,000 people in Leipzig, who parted before these techno prophets when they leapt off the stage. "That was really psycho, this was the future. But if we did it again, we wouldn't do it that hard, because life is hard enough."

Lit up in neon pink and surrounded by the gabber-converts they've made over the last five years of casual partying in Paris, bald-headed Paul Seul cues up the first track. Resident designer and recent DJ Claude Murder swills from a can of Heineken as MC Lucien Krampf in wraparound shades and peroxide mohawk garbles down a detuned mic. Tall moustachioed Evil Grim Grimace takes over, proudly dressed in Casual Gabberz merch to drop his own Frapcore bomb '3 Litres', and the Boiler Room goes off. There's the twinkling rushy e-synth reprieve of Paul's 'GVB' before it's into another banger, played by the next member handing over the headphones like a baton. By the time Von Bikräv and Evil Grim's 'R.A.G.E', drops, Krampf leaps onto the table, he can't contain it anymore, and we're only seven minutes in.

"I wanted to Brusselize Paris," Claude Murder explained to *Tsugi* about the origins of one of the most well known and underrated hardcore collectives of the streaming era. "I had an energy that was both destructive and reconstructive. I wanted to smash everything, dance everywhere and party for 72 hours."

In May 2014, this crew of hip hop heads unveiled their "casual" mission to the world. *Gabber Expo*, held at the multidisciplinary arts centre Point Ephémère on the Canal Saint-Martin, was the first major exhibition celebrating the cult and youth subculture of Dutch gabber with heritage objects and merch from Holland displayed alongside contemporary art projects like the iconic gabber fashion line from Dutch student Tom Nijhuis (turned into the iconic flashing blue gifs, as renowned amongst internet gabbers as the *Fusion mes Couilles* Boiler Room).

Since the *Gabber Expo*, rave culture has been exhibited at some of the most revered white cubes in the world, from 2019's *Sweet Harmony* at the Saatchi Gallery to *Expo Electro* held simultaneously at the Philharmonie de Paris. The latter was curated by Jean Yves Leloup, from seminal rave station Radio FG (involved in the first major Parisian techno exhibition, *Global Tekno*, held in 1995). The *Gabber Expo* nearly bankrupted its co-founders Paul and Maxime (Aprile), but it did launch the party collective (and sound) that would set the agenda for the hard dance revival of the internet generation.

"As our name suggests, we Casual Gabberz claim a relaxed take on the gabber," they announced on social media. "We come from different musical horizons but what unites us is an inherent love of the rave, hardcore and the gabber universe!"

Behind the carefree front of Casual Gabberz, social politics have been quietly driving the collective. "Someone told me the gabber scene is not racist in itself, but it's a scene where it's allowed to be racist," says Paul, "which is a big problem." He first encountered gabber culture whilst living in Amsterdam, becoming fascinated with the media stigma – "why do people think that gabbers are all skinheads? Is it real," mused Paul – and Mokum's counter sloganism and its United Gabbers Against Racism & Facism strapline, which has appeared on every vinyl release since 1993.

When the Dutch gabber scene collapsed, it was replaced by a new subculture and uniform look. Hardcore kids of the millennium ditched the colourful Australians and Nike trainers of the '90s, for Lonsdale shirts and rolled up jeans over army boots – provoking another, more damaging moral panic through the mid-'00s. The media were quick to make and exacerbate a link between warning Lonsdale clothing and right-wing extremism, as if the two were synonymous. After an escalation in racially-motivated incidents in Holland became conflated with this hardcore subculture, police and the national security service, AIVD, launched an investigation into the so-called Lonsdale Youth crisis. The AIVD discovered that only a small proportion of youths who wore the clothing brand actually held right-wing extremist beliefs, as *De Volkskrant* reported in July 2005, but the stigma endured.

In June 2005, during the peak of the media-inflamed Lonsdale Youth crisis, several hardcore promoters banded together to throw Hardcore United, a huge anti-racism event at Beursgebouw in Eindhoven, supported by DJs throughout the scene. All proceeds were donated to the National Bureau For Combating Racial Discrimination (LBR). The rise of right-wing extremism in Holland during this period, and the violence that came with it, did bleed into the hardcore scene, even if only a small minority followed the ideology.

"For gabbers that was a dark time," says Alberto Guerrini of his millennium hardcore scene in Italy. "Fascism, drug dealers, baby gangs, male only, bro-macho, you know the stereotype. When I started University and hanging out with people in the arts, I was ashamed to say [to them] that I was listening to hardcore." This was in 2005.

Alberto is best known for his stigma-appraising youth culture blog, Gabber Eleganza, which launched in 2011 as a way to reclaim his hardcore past from the typically damning media portrayals. Growing up in Bergamo in the North, with hardcore blasting from scooters and open windows, these Italian youth were never gabbers, they were Warriors. "We never said we dance to gabber music," Alberto explains. "We said hardcore, and it's still like that."

40 KM from Alberto's home town stands the most infamous gabber temple outside of Holland, where Italian Godfather Claudio Lancini has been rousing Italian *ultras* into a frenzy since the '90s with the hooligan hardcore of Rotterdam.

"I was thirteen when I found out about Number One," says Alberto about the kitschy neo-classic super disco in Corte Franca. "Older friends were talking about this club where everyone does the human pyramid, and for us it was like, what the fuck?"

The human pyramid formed Number One's closing ritual in the Sala 2, where ravers would scramble over each other during the last record to try and touch the ceiling of the 1,700-square-meter second room. Lancini has presided over Sala 2 since the early '80s, transitioning from playing commercial dance music with techno at the end, into full-throttle hardcore at his own Hardcore Warriors event, inaugurated in 1994 by Parkzicht's DJ Rob. Attendees became known as the Hardcore Warriors, evolving into its own subculture, exclusive to the club, through the decade.

Like the gabbers in Holland, Number One's Hardcore Warriors were instantly recognisable: hair glued up in colourful spikes and chunky buffalo platform shoes for height, the Joker-style face paint for comic intimidation, and fluro working jackets over ripped tights to amplify the working class heritage; with capoeira-type dance moves designed to clear a spot on the dancefloor.

The human pyramid morphed from a "moment of collective euphoria" into "a sort of guerrilla warfare," writes Federico Chiari in his history of Number One. When the lights came on, the dancefloor emptied in anticipation for the final track of the night – records like 'Oh Claudio, Play This Song' (produced by Lancini and protégé Jappo together with Lenny Dee for Industrial Strength). When the needle dropped, the dancefloor closed back up in a crush of bodies. Bruises, bloody faces and broken bones were worn with pride in this most extreme hardcore phenomena. "The atmosphere began to get heavy with the arrival of violent groups from the outskirts of Milan, especially from Pioltello, Cinisello Balsamo and Cologno Monzese," notes Chiari, who turned the finale into "an excuse to beat each other up."

The ecstasy-related death of nineteen-year-old Yannick Blesio on October 31, 1999, who died in hospital after attending a hardcore rave at the club, made national headlines, condemning the club and its Warrior subculture further. Number One closed down through the winter as it embarked on a lengthy trial that was won many years later.

Alberto's family banned him from going, but he went anyway, sneaking out to attend Number One's biggest hardcore event, Ravestorm, in early 2000, just as the Warrior subculture was emerging. He was only fifteen. "I still remember the emotion, the position where I was in the club," he recalls, gazing down on the black and white chequered floor from the maze of stairwells over the main floor. "I went in the afternoon, and was back home in time for dinner." His virgin ears were still reliving the music for days after.

Two decades later, Alberto is reanimating his youthful sense of wonder with the Hakke Show, an artistic representation of the Dutch gabber dance and the fetishised moves that every raver in Holland instinctively knows. "The Hakke seems very easy, but it's very difficult," says Alberto, who's the DJ during these performances, which have transitioned from the white cube gallery space into audiovisual stage takeovers at events like Amsterdam Dance Event, Sonar and Dour, with Alberto's tattooed gabber friends from Milan and Rotterdam showcasing their individual styles.

The Hakke Show, like the Gabber Eleganza blog, is unashamedly nostalgic. "I didn't want to do something new," Alberto explains. "It was about expressing my love for hardcore in a different environment" and premiered in summer 2016 at the Hangar Bicocca contemporary art museum in Milan during the Fara Fara Music Festival. Fara Fara, meaning face-to-face, is a Congolese sound clash with one group playing against another. Curated by exhibiting artist Carsten Höller, the festival was programmed with Lorenzo Senni, who booked Alberto to close his European side of the sound clash against Congolese group Les Anciens du Quartier Latin. Watching his gabber friends dancing in the crowd, inspiring others to become more engaged in his DJ set, and the music, encouraged Alberto to bring the Hakke Show to London and Club to Club in Turin the following summer, as Casual Gabberz debuted as a six-man "boy band" at Astropolis festival in Brest, playing for Manu Le Malin's hardcore Mekanik tent.

But Casual Gabberz were more than their gabber boy band image; they were activists and socialist too. Records and merch sales have been donated to charities providing aid for the escalating migrant crisis at the

French-UK border, and they became less "casual" and increasingly vocal about the underlying racism and xenophobia they were seeing in their scene.

Summer 2019 was a turning point, when the body of twenty-four-year-old Steve Maia Caniço was found in the River Loire near Nantes. He had been pushed into the water, along with up to fourteen others, and drowned during a police raid of a free Fête de la Musique rave. More police violence ensued during a vigil held in August that ended in riots and mass arrests. Casual Gabberz joined many others on social media calling out the cruel and excessive use of force by the French gendarmerie against ravers and activists.

During the pandemic Casual Gabberz released their most politicised record, 'Fuck Le 17', a hardcore bootleg of a renown French rap protest song (by Sevran), made into a *gilets jaunes* protest anthem through lockdown. It was issued as part of the *United Ravers Against Fascism EP* by Live From Earth Klub together with the Gabber Eleganza's Never Sleep label and intended to bring the original's "rage against state violence to techno parties." But instead of agitating their scene with activism, they were met with criticism. Elder Maxime stopped DJing, quitting Casual Gabberz entirely to join the *gilets jaunes* protest movement.

Over Christmas 2023, gabber's most casually radical collective announced they were disbanding. Paul had since moved to Brussels and formed the hyper hardcore pop act Ascendant Vierge with chanteuse singer-songwriter Mathilde Fernandez; feeling aged out and alienated from his Parisian pre-pandemic gabber scene. They dropped one last mega compilation, *Meilleurs Vœux (Forever)*, before signing off: Casual Gabberz Will Die, But You Won't.

GOD IS A GBBRGRL

14

It's Sunday Funday at the Walibi World theme park in middle Holland, and the bungee is going already. Fancy dress is encouraged, but most people are using their cardboard warrior costumes as self-made hats to shelter from these killer June rays. Strawberry-raw skin melds with the pineapple pyjamas and inflatable bananas at this hard dance Wonderland, which has taken more than 7,000 people three weeks to build up.

Defqon.1 started on a beach in Almere in 2003 with stages for techno, trance and young talents, as well as a platform for the hardstyle genre it had recently trademarked. Twenty years later, and the biggest harder styles festival in the world is attracting 250,000 visitors to engage in four days of experiential DJ music shows, whilst being pedaled 172 different merchandise products. There are secret super deluxe VIP lounges and viewing platforms, if you have the right wristband. You can get lost here, and not just in the music.

At the silverstage, a humble trailer surrounded by giant steampunk robots, the hardcore diehards brace against the UV beams to be eviscerated by the gorgeous feminine terror of Brooklyn-based Kilbourne. Even though she didn't start making hardcore, Ashe Kilbourne has been hardcore for most of her adolescence, gazing goggle-eyed at YouTube videos showing dirt bikes and confetti explosions and dudes dressed in plaid shirts pouring beer into their shoes.

Ashe first attended Defqon.1 in 2016 when hardcore was "bedroom music" – as in music she was consuming obsessively alone in her room. Seven years later, she has become a queer role model in the hardcore scene. At Defqon.1 she plays tracks from her upcoming PRSPCT release, but also music by her new core peers, like French industrial artist RaBBeAT, who opens the Silverstage, and is in the crowd raving along with the rest.

"Nothing has made me feel so unleashed and excited before," she explains. "There's something so flamboyant about a lot of hardcore. The earth-shattering drums into this over the top supersaw synth lead to these over-declared statements, and then back into the drop, it reminds me of musicals. It's really high-drama music."

In 2019 Kilbourne signed to Industrial Strength Records with *NJ Terror*, her homage to the electronic punk sound that used to reverberate through the neighbourhood where she now lives. Containing four tracks of buzzsaw speedcore with guitar riffs and screamo vocals, it shows Kilbourne's sensitivity and self-awareness as a third generation artist moving through this scene, whose filtering steeped history through her own lens to create a sound that feels genuine and purist, but also exciting and fresh. "I really do want to try to be faithful to whatever my understanding of this music is," she says.

Between the 2016 self-released records, *Sourland* and *18 Songs*, Kilbourne transitioned from the bricolage sound of KUNQ to the new core artist she's been ever since. "With *Sourland*, I wasn't thinking about genre or form as much as wanting to try and write something that felt expressive of the head state I was in," she says. The EP processes intense feelings of trauma, violence and physical pain, all of which are intimately connected to Kilbourne's experiences as a queer trans woman.

Kilbourne's personal and musical identities are inextricably bound, and she delivers her fiercely felt politics in calm and considered tones. She discovered club music as she was starting to feel trans and living in a queer house during her freshman year, throwing explicitly queer parties in frat houses. Kilbourne's music remains politically aware and socially engaged, even though she acknowledges the limitations of activism within a nightclub context. "It's really important to have dance music that empowers marginalised people and communities," she says, "but I also have a more sober view now that this isn't undoing structural racism and misogyny and classism."

While living in Connecticut, Kilbourne started playing guitar and writing lyrics. She formed the grindcore band PYKA with two friends, culminating in the Bandcamp album *Too Femme Too Furious*. Other hardcore band projects followed, like Ghüla, a punk four-piece featuring Kilbourne on drums, and the "ecstatic grindcore" group Trophy Hunt. There's also Cicada, which evolved during a stint in New Orleans, where Kilbourne relocated after graduating from Wesleyan. The track 'Honey' from *NJ Terror* is dedicated to Kilbourne's former Cicada bandmate, who sadly passed away. Opening with washes of melancholic synths and moody breakbeats, it's a beautiful example of how vulnerable this style of dance music can be.

"As a queer and trans person, one of the basic aspects of those identities is a feeling of outsiderness at some point in your life," says Ashe. "In high school, I didn't feel such a difference between liking grindcore and punk. I imagine there's a similar story for a lot of people looking for extreme sounds, for sounds that are weird and fucked up, because being trans or being gay is an alienating experience at times."

The wounded tenderness lingering beneath Kilbourne's brutal sound design lends the music its potency. She uses hardcore's heightened drama and strength to present a softer, more fragile side in counterpoint. And in bearing both sides of herself with honesty and authenticity to the world, she's encouraged others to step up and queerify the hardcore boys' club.

Another Dutch summer later, and the Netherlands is making hard dance history again. On July 20, 2024, Amsterdam's Johan Cruyff ArenA – home of Ajax and the national football team – hosted "the world's BIGGEST hard techno rave" by Verknipt. They sold out this 40,000 capacity stadium venue within weeks of the first announcement, without releasing a single name on the bill.

The Dutch techno brand has been selling its concept of total raving freedom to enthusiastic youth for a decade; rebranding as the dominant force of hard techno since 2022, with a big room soundtrack to match their no rules, no boundaries mantra. Hard techno according to Verknipt is a chaotic mashup of any and all genres, from psytrance and sing along pop hooks, to the most sledgehammer hardcore possible. Sets are emotionally wrought and high-impact, propelled by a galloping rumble kick. It's disruptive and dynamic, nostalgically nodding to the past, whilst simultaneously ripping up all the rules, delivered in a high-tech multi-sensorial explosion of lasers, strobes and video projections.

Overshadowed by the more established Dutch techno events, such as Awakenings, Verknipt couldn't compete with "the big guys" when they started in 2012, so they had to create their own scene, booking new talents and previously unknown names outside of Verknipt, that have turned into the stadium superstars of the 2020s.

Verknipt's elevation of the humble warehouse experience into dazzling audiovisual shows made them a go-to for rave-hungry youth during the pandemic, when the dance industry moved online. Verknipt events, which have been live streamed and loaded up to YouTube since 2017, have been the fodder for Gen Z to encounter a lockdown-prohibited rave culture, made all the more enticing by the taboo.

"Many people called us lucky during COVID," stated Verknipt's general manager Michelle Verhoef. "But you also have to dare to take the risk." The brand's rapid expansion through the pandemic has been the driver to become even more ambitious with their production scope and scale: "The moment your events get bigger, you are commercial," Verhoef stated, "because we're already commercial, it's OK to be more commercial. Let's see how it works."

"If you ask our audience who Jeff Mills is, a lot of people probably don't know," co-founder and chief booker Mer Hajbarati admitted to *3voor12*. Verknipt's audience aren't so invested in the history of rave culture. They just want to rave. "There are many parties that still like to book that type of artist, but that doesn't attract the young target group."

Verknipt's ArenA debut pivoted around an epic scripted and time-coded Experience Show, crafted in amped-up tribute to Sensation, Holland's flagship trance rave that launched the careers of DJs Tiësto and Armin van Buren from this very venue through the millennium. No expense was spared then to make Sensation "a visual spectacle," writes Gert van Veen in *Release / Celebrate Life: The Story of ID&T*, "more grandiose than all other events"; where the DJs were "supporting acts" to Cirque du Soleil-inspired performances set to pre-recorded megamixes, with every segment introduced by a voice over – the sultry tones of famous American voice actor, John. B. Wells. Verknipt recreated the formula with drummers, plumes of fire and aerialists lit up by more than 500 lights and lasers. It's a social media moment, to film and be filmed, captured by 40,000 smartphones raised high.

Austin native Sara Landry played the primetime slot. Crowned the "World's No.1 Hard DJ" by *DJ Mag* in their 2024 end of year polls, Landry has leaned into her media credentials as the "Queen" of the scene. She ends her Verknipt performance with a trio of teasers from her self-released debut album, *Spiritual Driveby*, released four months after ArenA. It's a savvy piece of marketing from an artist who's playing the post-pandemic hard techno game.

Sara Landry is one of just two women acts on the 2024 ArenA bill.

Hard techno is just another hard dance boys club. "It's still extremely tilted towards men," says Kilbourne after her experiences at Defqon.1, where she was one of the few women on a lineup of more than 500 artists. "The femininity picked up by these organisations is very narrow and traditionally 'feminine,'" she says. Ashe is authentically challenging gender norms with her sensitive hardcore productions, like her *Milkshake EP* for PRSPCT featuring the aptly-titled 'Sunshine Terror'. "Terror is often so one-note," she explains. "It's just angry, angry, angry, and 'Milkshake' is a really fun song."

Hard dance has always been big in the Benelux: a literal mass movement since Thunderdome packed 30,000 ravers into an ice rink on its first outing. It has kept on expanding, getting more sensational and experience-driven in the decades since. The Lowlands have turned rave culture into a multimillion dollar global entertainment industry, and hard techno is the next evolution, with Verknipt at the most commercial end of the scale.

Hard techno isn't short of criticism. Perhaps the biggest issue is the name. Musically, it rejects techno's traditional traits, from the seamless trance-inducing mix to the all-black uniformed anonymity that once defined the culture, especially in Berlin. Verknipt's definition is deliberately broader and more ambiguous. "It's everything, plus techno," as GM Michelle Verhoef described it. Even Beatport aren't calling it "hard techno", adopting the term "neo-rave" for its latest channel dedicated to this newer, pop-coded sound – which they borrowed directly from Bang Face.

As a decentralised social media-molded movement, hard techno is upending traditional power structures and enabling anyone to be the next DJ superstar. But this has also created even more pressure for artists to become personas instead of musicians, and to conform to the new post-pandemic industry rules, where artists are brands, DJs are influencers, and content teams are mandatory, if you want to keep your spot in an ever-shrinking limelight.

"Social media is not a choice, it's a necessity, if you want to be successful," stated the *BBC* broadcaster Frank McWeeny whilst moderating a panel about *The Art of Exponential Growth* with "psy-techno" star Indira Paganotto in 2023, who has documented her superstar rise and jetsetter DJ life in the vlog series, *On the Road with Indira Paganotto*.

"There's a higher churn rate of artists than before," confirms Somniac One, a multifaceted producer from the industrial hardcore scene who has been blowing up in hard techno after lockdown (without a content team). "The artists are more temporary, the stars are more temporary."

Somniac One started making bedroom music in 2005, breaking through a decade later signed to PRSPCT with a series of thoughtful club bangers that are as intelligent and approachable as the studio nerd behind the witty social media presence. *Troubled Youth* and the prescient track 'Shirtless' alluded to hardcore's bro culture with a wink when it was released in 2017. It has become even more potent post-lockdown, as a comment on a scene once powered by sound-and-body interactions alone. The artwork is a carefully constructed collage of women representing themselves on social media, wasted at parties or baring their flesh, with cutesy internet graphics obscuring their faces.

Somniac One has never been a fan of the limelight, but she is embracing it to be an ambassador for the nicher core-oriented styles under the commercial hard dance umbrella. As Verknipt was building up the ArenA, she was in Berlin presenting her Somniverse label in the strobing concrete womb of Tresor. Her lineup included introverted flashscore artist Neurocore, known for his gorgeous high-velocity techno, some of it so fast it becomes an ambient sound bath, and Sunshine Terrorist Kilbourne.

"There were techno fans, industrial techno fans, hardcore fans, and also these true Berlin ravers, naked people dancing in the front to Neurocore," she recalls. "People were there for the music."

Somniac One performed the closing ritual behind those iconic iron bars where the original '90s hard techno culture gestated, and endures today in the underground club institutions facilitating meaningful encounters with music – and people. "It's really important for me to connect with the community in one way or another," she continues. "There's more to being a member of this scene than DJing and making music. That's also where I see the light in the current darkness – with the people who do their thing wholeheartedly."

Around her Defqon.1 debut, Ashe launched her own Hammerhead party series as an incubator for NYC's new core community. "Friends came early and helped put up decorations and get the space ready," she says about the first edition at H0L0 in Queens. Somniac One made her New York debut headlining the first party of 2024, with the fifth Hammerhead taking place six months later during Pride. "Gay gabbers link up" was the call to arms and featured local talent Áine Suekwei, involved behind the scenes from the start, warming up for Dutch guests the Outside Agency and Mindustries.

These grassroots initiatives, with women pushing women, is how the "his-story" of hardcore can turn into a "her-story," as Bianca Ludewig explained, a hardcore scholar and member of the female:pressure network, who wrote her master thesis on hardcore and breakcore in Berlin. "Other scholars, like Tara Rodgers, have shown how women are getting systematically written out of music history," says Bianca, "and as a woman you need some inspiration through role models to show that it's normal as a woman to be a DJ or musician."

Beyond the Dutch stadium raves, crew culture and collectivism has been a significant tool for this new generation to get ahead, by supporting and encouraging one another. In the case of Drömfakulteten in Stockholm, this has resulted from working side-by-side in the same studio space – a water-damaged, airless basement they've since had to vacate – where its twelve musically variegated members have learned their craft together. "A lot of us would have stopped," says founder Katja Lindeberg, who performs barbed sets with pointed shark teeth painted across her face as HAJ300. "We have really depended on being able to speak to each other and share experiences."

Harder styles FLINTA (female, lesbian, inter, non-binary, trans and agender people) crews have been bubbling to the fore on either side of the pandemic. They include Belgium safespace ravers Burenhinder, and Explity Music in Paris. There's also Amsterdam-based Hard Attack, promoted by vinyl DJs Gysèle and Akemio Grey, which has programming established scene names alongside upcoming locals, with a focus on women artists since April 2023: "I see so many great young girls playing early rave," says Gysèle, "and mostly playing vinyl, too. They deserve a big stage in our opinion." Women behind the scenes as bookers and club managers and promoters, like Gysèle, are needed to further tip the scales.

FLINTA producers have also been changing the sound of hardcore, which doesn't mean cheesy pop song vocals over hard kicks. The Explity Music label was inaugurated at the start of 2023 with a compilation of sweetly-distorted club bangers and bedroom listening music. "It's important for us to build bridges between different musical genres," explains co-founder KimberlaID, who weaves scintillating pastel synths and cool bluesy melodies through her tough digital kicks. "As someone said, God is a Girl Gabber," she continues, "and we want to make room for gender minorities in the industry: we're more and more visible, but still not enough."

The responsibility should not just fall on the shoulders of the young – or the women. Change needs to happen from within the scene, which is already taking place at the smaller club level in Rotterdam, where '90s teen DJ Dennis "Panic" Copier is programming young, upcoming (and female) acts for his Panic Room parties at Perron. Meanwhile, Energiehal raver Leonie has become the vinyl DJ Lady Error since turning her bedroom into an internet streaming station during lockdown: "I really want the new generation to get that old pure hardcore gabber feeling through my music," she says.

The hardcore dance industry has changed dramatically since Leonie started going to gabber raves, aged fourteen. And the music has changed too. What hasn't changed is the community core of hardcore: of gabbers standing up for their gabbers. "Gabber was always a genre for marginals and outsiders of all sorts," says other Explity co-founder Talita, "so it makes sense that this music stays a soundtrack for our struggles."

"Hardcore is a feeling," Ashe concludes. "It's wonderful alone in the bedroom" – she says in reference to her solitary teen entry into the scene – "and even more wonderful experienced with the people you love."

OUTRO: JOIN A CVLT!

The Maassilo glows like a fuchsia beacon in the pitch black November night as moonlight dances off a giant disco ball hovering over the shimmering Maas. A line has started to form as excited French, German and English chatter mingle in the frosty air. "Take my picture," shouts a long-haired American. Basecek is standing beside the PRSPCT XL poster with his Breakcore Gives Me Wood warriors, bearded Andrew Slave To Society, and skinny Limewax, disguised in shades and hoodie, who all played together in Belgium the night before. "This is my Thunderdome!" Baseck proudly declares.

Baseck is the newest member of the PRSPCT family, although chief Thrasher has been a fanboy for years. Usually he's backstage during these big end of year blowouts, but tonight he's corralling everyone to go see the ultimate punk rock jungle activist from LA, who delivers his battle-hardened liveset whilst grindcore-screaming down the mic.

But Hellfish is up first, DJing happy hardcore in Secret Squirrel guise, sporting a bucket hat and more of a grin than usual from the curmudgeonous Deathchant chief. His "Rice" partner Akira and entourage (including son and terror protegee Bruhze) sit in the wings. Next to Bang Face, PRSPCT is the spiritual home of Deathchant, with mainstays Producer and Dolphin releasing their funky UK hardcore and trippier technological techno across both labels, which have become more twisted and entwined since Thrasher issued the most Deathchant EP on Deathchant in years.

Producer plays back to back with Dolphin in the PRSPCT XTRM Area, transforming this concrete industrial cathedral in Holland's harbour city into the sweaty sweatbox of the Technodrome. Then Manu Le Malin mounts the stage to commandeer the rave with Somniac One, who breach the generational divide with mutual respect and a shared musical vision that burns through the boundaries of techno and hardcore.

The PRSPCT XL crowd is as mixed as the music: free party tekno heads with dreads dance next to the Australian-wearing second generation gabbergirls and the topless hard techno boys. There's lots of Bang Face Hard Crew, plus steam punks and wizards, leopard print onesies and alien backpacks, and Number One Italian Warrior clown faces. And everyone is moving and mingling between the stages. It's the Breaking Barriers dream that Andre van Zuijlen had for Thunderdome in 2010, realised and functioning across three uniquely distinct, diverse and symbiotic floors. PRSPCT's vision of hardcore has never lived inside boxes.

"We're not trying to chase this trend, or jump on the wagon; we've got our own fucking wagon," as chief Gareth de Wijk explained to *DJ Mag* about his anti-business business model, derived from years sleeping on floors and living out of vans playing in bands in the DIY punk scene. "The way we treat the artists, the way we treat our music, what we love about it, the attitude of it is all super punk – it's just super DIY, fuck the rules."

PRSPCT artists have the freedom to be their weirdest, most radical selves. Back in the basement, the label's first teenage fuck-the-rules producer Limewax plays angular and shattered Warp techno from a laptop. This extremely introverted music clears the floor of hedonists for Andy Slave To Society to fill back up again, which has been his post-pandemic challenge since quitting his career-defining techno act AnD.

AnD were the hardest of the 2010s British industrial techno revolution, who reintroduced gabber kicks to the techno bigroom. "It's all about getting hard man, harder and harder and harder" partner Dimitri declared to *Little White Earbuds* as the pair reinvented their Mancunian post-dubstep techno sound with heavy hardcore distortion and Go Hard or Go Home attitude.

"We were at the end of the minimal cycle and starting to get bored of the Berghain sound," says Andy, "and we felt like we could stand out by making subtle (or not so subtle) changes, moving back towards the Birmingham sound and '90's Tresor releases that we all loved – with hardcore."

Blowing off a successful techno career to play undanceable dance music on the grimy basement scene is the ultimate punk move, which Andy made just before lockdown. Motivated to make people move, whilst "perplexing" them at the same time, he's an experimental outlier amongst the outliers, which is as breakcore as it gets.

PRSPCT have been fucking up the Dutch hard dance industry for decades with stage takeovers at all the major spectacle-driven outdoor festivals, from Dominator to Decibel. PRSPCT are usually bundled up with Akira and his Hong Kong Violence band of saboteurs, and relegated to the literal outskirts, hidden in the woods, in tiny trailers so small the roof has to be sawn off for the DJs to fit. But that's fine, the diehards don't mind an adventure to seek out the hardcore perversions that no other stage dares to play.

Away from the sales and business speak of the lifestyle brands, sheltered from the social media fakes of the clubbing-as-entertainment industry, a more authentic diehard community continues to grow. These artists are not competing against each other for slots, and the legends are placed on the same pedestal as the young talents. Here, women perform side by side with the men, on the mainstage. This isn't a boys club, it's a PRSPCT club. But if you want in, you have to go all the way.

What is hardcore? It's PRSPCT. It's total beyond flesh and reason commitment: blood in, blood out, dance til you drop to your knees, to the floor, to the furnace, to the worms and the earth. Hardcore is wanting to quit but refusing to give up or give in. It's persisting through ill health, seeing a doctor and ignoring the advice, to push through the breakdowns, the breakups, and synaptic traumas, for the sake of the mission, for the cause, because there's nothing else outside of this. Nothing else matters.

Hardcore is bankruptcy, homelessness, and addiction – and having your hardcore family there to pull you through. It's not about money or fame or the limelight, even when this happens. And it does, because hardcore is basement music, playing to the concrete walls and empty floors, whilst simultaneously packing out stadiums shot through with lasers. It's performing for yourself, and the twisting contorting masses, who show their loyalty by donning uniformed outfits: colourful tracksuits and trainers; all-black or military camouflage; boots and hoodies; leather bondage gear, or no clothes at all.

Hardcore relics have been passed down unchanged through the generations, from fathers to sons, and mothers to daughters, who can't wait to share the best moments of their youth with their children, who they hope will grow up as rebellious as them. Hardcore will never die because it has been tattooed onto the bodies of millions, and fused to the soul. It has burrowed to a place so deep it's too dangerous to be cut out, so you just have to live with it. Hardcore is not a pebble in your shoe, it's the burn on your cornea that you cannot unsee. It sees you.

We are immortalised in distorted kicks, raving on this plane of oblivion as the planet grinds to dust. Darkness is not mystical, it's your everyday reality, as the first hardcore techno prophet once said. So let's not mourn this stupid human drama, this somnambulist existence, the eternal living death of life. Instead, let's party like it's our last. Let's Dance, or Die. Hardcore.

APPENDIX

PHOTO CREDITS

1.1 PCP in Frankfurt, 1992 / Acardipane Archive

1.2 Tresor club on the Leipziger Strasse Berlin / Tresor Archive

1.3 Tresor club opening on the Leipziger Strasse Berlin, 1991 / Tresor Archive

2.1 Hard Wax advert from *Frontpage* magazine, 1992

2.2 Underground Resistance flyer for the RoXY Amsterdam, 1992

2.3 Underground Resistance at Tresor club on the Leipziger Strasse Berlin, 1991 / Submerge Detroit and Tresor Archive

3.1 Spiral Tribe communiqué London, 1992 / Spiral Tribe Archive

3.2 DJ Warlock Pulse FM cassette London / Warlock Archive

3.3 *Ravescene* magazine, 1992 / Warlock Archive

3.4 Ixy, Debbie and Jeckle the dog on the road, 1998 / Spiral Tribe Archive

3.5 Postcard from Keith Desert Storm, 1998 / Spiral Tribe Archive

4.1 VFM at the Vox London flyer, 1994 / VFM Archive

4.2 Colin Dale at Knowledge London, 1993 / Daniel Newman for DJ Mag

4.3 Jason VFM at Club Essence London, 1995 / VFM Archive

4.4 Save the 121 street party flyer London, 1999 / urban75

4.5 Live Evil IX flyer London, 2004

6.1 Liza N Eliaz in Berlin, 1995 / Tilman Brembs zeitmaschine.org

7.1 Planet E flyer Amsterdam, 1989

7.2 Waxweazle in the studio Rotterdam / Waxweazle Archive

7.3 Rotterdam gabberhouse at Parkzicht / DJ Rob and ID&T Archive

8.1 Rotterdam gabber Leonie with *Exactitudes* by Ari Versluis, 2024 / Dennis van Rijswijk

9.1 Hellway to Mokum flyer Amsterdam, 1996
9.2 Disciples of Annihilation for Inner Rhythm at the Fubar Stirling, 1995 / Martin Langer
9.3 Q-Tex on the cover of *M8* magazine, 1994

10.1 Bunker Spezial Sylvester flyer Berlin, 1992
10.2 Alle im Eimer flyer Berlin, 1999
10.3 Nordcore at the Box flyer Hamburg, 1996
10.4 Tresor club closing party on the Leipziger Strasse Berlin, 2005 / Tresor Archive

11.1 Mysteryland Winter Edition Utrecht, 1997 / Mirko Kuit for ID&T Archive
11.2 Dana / ID&T Archive
11.3 Københardcore street propaganda Copenhagen / KBHC Archive
11.4 Copenhagen gabbers / KBHC Archive

13.1 Gabber Eleganza presents the Hakke Show at Dour / Frankie Casillo
13.2 Marc Acardipane / Acardipane Archive
13.3 *ESS* (*Entretenir Surveiller Sécuriser*) artwork, 2018 / Paul Seul and Casual Gabberz

14.1 *Milkshake EP* artwork, 2023 / Kilbourne and PRSPCT Recordings
14.2 *Rendered Fat EP* artwork, 2020 / Somniac One and PRSPCT Recordings
14.3 DJ Gysèle at the Melkweg Amsterdam, 2023 / Hard Attack
14.4 Tresor club on the Köpenicker Strasse Berlin / Camille Blake for Tresor Archive

HARDCORE TERMINOLOGY

ARDKORE / HARDCORE RAVE / NUT NUT HARDCORE

"Hardcore means different things to different people, and they're all correct," as London pirate radio legend Jason Warlock states. In *Generation Ecstasy*, Simon Reynolds defined hardcore in dance music as "scenes where druggy hedonism and underclass desperation combine with a commitment to the physicality of dance and a no-nonsense functionalist approach to making music ("tracks" rather than "songs".)" Hardcore in Britain referred to the rave scene between 1990 and 1993, before splintering into jungle and techno. '92 was the year of nut nut mental ardkore, culminating in the week-long Castlemorton Common Free Festival held in the Malvern Hills in Worcestershire, over the May Bank Holiday. Spiral Tribe were the hardcore of the ardkore.

BREAKCORE

The genre that is not a genre, breakcore is anything that's not four-four. Freely distributed via p2p software and debated on forums, it was the first post-rave scene to embrace the cyberpunk utopia of the internet. Coined in Germany by Tanith with a short lived Break Core party series in '92; Dead By Dawn in London were playing it without naming it, and ferried it over to Europe with the tekno-nomad sound systems. But it was claimed by American junglists, Milwaukee's Doormouse and Baseck from LA, who aligned with Ed Duran Duran Duran and Pete Dev/Null from Philly to blaze a breakbeat trail across the states. "Breakcore is activism, togetherness, and punk rock jungle," says Baseck, who crafted breakcore on a gameboy before becoming a hardware master. "What is Breakcore? It means the ability to experiment," stated Doormouse after releasing his 2022 comeback EP, *Breakcore*. "It means unpredictability and sweet, sweet chaos."

BOUNCY TECHNO / TARTAN TECHNO

Banging Rotterdam gabber fused with piano-riffy happy hardcore played to white-gloved Scottish ravers under the big top tents of Rezerection between '94 and '97. Bouncy techno was the nut nut hardcore scene of Scotland twinning with Holland, with cartoony colour and silly sounds, sped up in the ecstasy rush of the last liberated years of rave.

CHEAPCORE

The underground "nosebleed" sound of Newcastle Australia's Bloody Fist label, Max Death from London's Squcide Squad collective, and anyone else making breakbeat-driven basement music with an Atari or early Apple Macintosh computer. Named by Nasenbluten with their *Cheapcore EP* on Strike Records in '97, it was never intended for the megaraves. In his preface to *Fistography*, cataloguing the Bloody Fist label, Mark writes of their first 12" *Newcastle Hardcore Volume One*: "It sounded like shit and nothing about it could be considered deep or even remotely sophisticated." It was anti-chinstroke music, hand stamped and paid with doll money, and veined with an obnoxious attitude. "We let all our aggression out on the computer. Instead of killing people, we do it with sound," as Mark N explained to Simon Reynolds in *Generation Ecstasy*.

DOOMCORE / GLOOMCORE

The frozen "sick ambient" sound of PCP's Marc Acardipane and Miro pushing the Mescalinum United blueprint beyond the apocalypse. "Imagine surveying earth after nuclear destruction and enjoying what you see, that's how it feels when you listen to it," as Marc explained to *Alien Underground* in 1995. After an ecstasy overdose and experiencing the darkside of NYC's Limelight rave scene, around this time Oliver Chesler combines his Industrial Strength Temper Tantrum sound with his EBM goth roots to become the Horroist.

GABBA

The English bastardisation of gabber, generally used in the '90s by (outsider) media and journalists, including Simon Reynolds.

GABBER

The Dutch hardcore rave music of the '90s, and affiliated youth movement. The subculture continues relatively untouched, whilst the music has been reinvented in the 2010s neo-gabber scene. Gabber music is specific, even though it has become interchangeable with hardcore. In '94, Christophe Fringeli described gabber in *Alien Underground* magazine as "simplistic, energetic, humourous, and highly controversial." Danish neo-gabber, Peckerhead, has updated the sound, but kept true to the gabber core.

FRAPCORE

Parisian crew Casual Gabberz and their definitive pairing of French lyric rap music with a harder styles mashup of genres – or hardcore for the internet generation.

FRENCHCORE

Radium biographer, journalist and Parisian speedcore promoter Florian Pittion-Rossillon explains: "The original benchmark of the Frenchcore sound is the track 'Noise Theater' by Micropoint, released in late 1998 on vinyl album *Neurophonie*. There were precursors before this track, but this one crystallises the formula," which he describes as a kick with a dry attack, and a distorted offbeat bass. "But it's not just a matter of the kick, even if it is very characteristic," he adds. French Hardcore of the '90s – "industrial, cold, abstract, often proto-Terror," says Florian – is not the bouncy, silly teknival Frenchcore of the early 2000s.

FLASHCORE

"The most avant-garde form of hardcore" according to reddit, Flashcore is the high-velocity hardcore closely associated with the French Hangars Liquides label and its founder, La Peste; updated by Neurocore and his exquisitely nerdy sound baths. The (all caps) Hangars Liquides manifesto states: "Flashcore is the spatial and temporal conception of air landscapes of which 'sonic atoms' (the smallest particle of sound which is thought as an entity in itself) are being controlled with the exclusive aim of making us explore our minds and perceive any kind of transcendence." It was about pushing hardcore beyond the idea of harmony and rhythm, and maximising the potentiality of new music software.

HAPPY HARDCORE / HAPPY GABBER

One of the first distinctly UK music styles to emerge from the ardkore rave scene, according to *Red Bull Music Academy Daily,* with manic tempos and a cartoon aesthetic, steeped in childhood nostalgia, happy hardcore was innovated by Slipmatt and amped up to cheery colourful excess in the Midlands and Scotland, after bouncy techno banged itself out. When happy hardcore arrived in the Netherlands in the summer of 95, DJ Paul and Technohead topped the Dutch charts with their catchy Europop hits, serving as panacea for the first gabber crisis. Also known as happy gabber when combined with gabber kicks, the Rotterdam happy scene had a more sinister side, from Ruffneck and his breakbeat-driven "artcore" to the neurotic sound of Waxweazle.

HARDCORE

Over three decades, hardcore has evolved into a catchall term covering a wide range of harder styles music, from sludgy doomcore (at 60 to 140 BPM) to the goofy-aggressive terror (between 190 and 300 BPM) and faster, harsher speedcore. In the Netherlands, these have calcified beyond musical styles into discrete scenes and tribes, with their own infrastructure of events, artists and labels. Gabber is not part of the post-'90s Dutch hardcore umbrella. In other countries, hardcore is hardcore and can also mean gabber (it's complicated!) "Hardcore is for everyone, gabber is not," as astutely summarised by Peckerhead.

HARD DANCE

Hard dance is the commercial harder styles event industry, pioneered from the Benelux in the '90s and exported worldwide. It's also a more crew-based and nebulous internet mashup of hard club music, presented on the Boiler Room Hard Dance platform since 2019.

HARDCORE DRUM 'N' BASS / PRSPCT

Not to be confused with the Outside Agency and their crossbreed sound (a term started as an industry troll, that stuck). Even though TOA members (also in drum 'n' bass solo guise as DJ Hidden and Eye-D) are closely affiliated with PRSPCT, hardcore drum 'n' bass is the sound of Thrasher fucking with the two genres he loved and grew up with as an English-born Dutchman. "I met this kid who was relentless, and super stubborn to bring only the hard side of drum 'n' bass – and he made it big time," founding PRSPCT family member Adi-J told *DJ Mag*.

HARDSTYLE

A separatist subgenre pioneered by the Prophet and Dana after the Dutch gabber scene collapsed, combining techno, trance and UK hard house at an early hardcore tempo of 140 to 150 BPM. It was picked up by Wouter Tavecchio and Wildrik Timmerman at Q-Dance, trademarked on July 4, 2002, and grown into one of Holland's biggest dance music exports. Hardstyle started raw and underground when Dana was playing it at Multigroove, but Q-Dance made it a lifestyle brand for the masses.

HARDCORE TECHNO

Techno was born hardcore – with Jeff Mills playing Tresor in '91. Hardcore techno is techno music played by the hard core: the artists who live and die for techno, which includes Manu Le Malin (as The Driver) but also Luke DJ Producer and Tanith (when he feels like it). Somniac One is playing hardcore techno in the commercial 2020s hard techno scene (which has nothing to do with hardcore or techno...see below). 'We have Arrived' is the first and unanimously definitive Alpha and Omega of hardcore techno.

HARD TECHNO

A 2020s social media-driven rave culture and lifestyle, capitalised by Dutch techno brand Verknipt since 2022, filling stadiums with its no rules, no boundaries, hard dance music dialled up to 11. Hard techno has turned into the biggest global rave movement since Dutch gabber and UK hardcore of the '90s.

HARTCORE

'90's German fad for hardcore – the 't' making it even harder. Hart meaning hard, but also more dedicated, devoted, diehard.

INDUSTRIAL

The slower, darker, burning soul of underground hardcore, often played from the smallest stage at any Dutch hardcore event, or inside German concrete bunkers.

MILLENNIUM HARDCORE

Shiny, digital and bombastic hardcore from the 2000s suited to the new plugin and internet-driven digital native generation.

NEO-RAVE

The singular "explosion" of acid, jungle, rave hardcore, drum 'n' bass, breakcore, bass, techno and electronica, defined by James Saint Acid's record bag and his kaleidoscopic UK rave Bang Face from late 2003. Two decades later, neo-rave was adopted by Beatport to delineate the pop-coded harder styles music that has erupted out of lockdown from the platform's founding hard techno sound (schranz). Neo-rave brought the fun back to partying in London in the mid-00s; 2020s neo-rave inherits the same party-first vibe, delivered on a stadium-sized and internet-streamed scale.

NOSEBLEED

The name of Scottish promoter David Smit's hardcore residency at Visions, formerly Moist, held in a converted cinema venue in Rosyth, between summer '95 and '98. These parties regularly booked the Industrial Strength roster, but also DJ Smurf and his terror-pop music. Nosebleed is also a differential term between the early free party sound systems: you were either "fluffy" (house) or "nosebleed" (hardcore breakbeat-techno). Spiral Tribe producer and live performer Simon Crystal Distortion played across both, just to be different.

PSYCORE / PSYCHEDELIC HARDCORE

The blend of dark hardcore, breakbeat, tekno, acidcore, and psytrance, also called the "Cenobite sound" after the Dutch label by Mokum affiliate Tellurian, founded in 1996; updated by Peckerhead in Copenhagen in the 2010s.

SCHRANZ

The original hard and distorted runaway train of techno, set to a chugging 140 to 160 BPM, coined by Chris Liebing in the mid-'90s and popularised by acts like DJ Rush, Miss Djax and PETDuo through the '00s.

SPEEDCORE

A harsher, faster (200 and 300 BPM) distorted version of hardcore, infused with metal guitar riffs and a punk rock attitude in the NYC version – or straight up grindcore in the UK, as popularised by Loftgroover. The New York City speedcore sound of DOA, Temper Tantrum, and Delta 9 was specific but musically wide-ranging; the sound of a music family who didn't define themselves by BPMs. As core member Maria 909 explains: "Industrial Strength was a way of life. It was a motley crew of dysfunctionality and we were around each other all the time. Lenny gave kids that didn't fit a mold a new space to grow sonically, who needed a different distorted kick drum to dance to."

TEKNO

Free tekno, freetekno or just tekno, sometimes hardtek, pioneered by Spiral Tribe members Seb and Simon when they formed R-Zac from their mobile recording studio trailer, parked up in the frozen wastes of Potsdamer Platz, Berlin, before forwarding the revolution through Europe. It's dark, progressive and can go on forever, best experienced in a field after several days of not sleeping.

TERROR

One of the oldest and most aggressive hardcore subgenres, terror is also silly and spoofy. It's fast (190 to 300 BPM) and bludgeoning, with a few notable jesters, like the goblin-masked Noisekick. It formalised from a catchall term for the unclassifiable hardcore of the '90s into a fully-formed scene in the Netherlands around the The Tunnel Of Terror, popularised by "Opa" Drokz and partner in crime Akira. How does Akira define terror? "Terror is terrible."

TERRORCORE / SCARECORE

A more serious German (and early French) take on terror and gabber, forged in claustrophobic concrete bunkers beneath relentless strobes. It's the *Hartcore* of German hardcore, punishing and brutal, with all the Dutch gabber colour and silliness stripped away. Like all hardcore, it's best described as a feeling than defined by musical properties. UK legend Loftgroover coined scarecore on his self-released records in '95 (produced together with Vince Watson).

UK HARDCORE

Deathchant and the four-four hardcore sound of the Helter Skelter Technodrome room, as breakbeat rave was turning into drum 'n' bass in the mainroom. "UK hardcore was all about the funk and the groove from kicks, with that drive from breakbeats," explains Deathchant member Dolphin, who signed to PRSPCT in the 2010s. UK hardcore is a hip hop-derived, sample-digging, battle-turntablism scene, and the UK techno underground reclaiming its breakbeat core, as Luke Producer explains: "As much as I have techno in my life, and we use that to great effect to disrupt the scene and make people realise there is a difference, breakbeats are in my blood, man."

DIEHARD BIBLIOGRAPHY

Alwyn W. Turner – *A Classless Society: Britain in the 1990s* (Aurum, 2013)

Arne van Terphoven – *Multigroove* (Mary Go Wild, 2018)

Arne van Terphoven – *Thunderdome* (Mary Go Wild, 2018)

Arne van Terphoven – *Wat de Fok Ouwe* (Mary Go Wild, 2016)

Bianca Ludewig – *Utopie und Apokalypse in der Popmusik* (Verlag des Instituts für Europäische Ethnologie, 2019)

Bill Brewster – *Last Night A DJ Saved My Life* (Headline, 2006)

Bloody Fist – *Fistography* (Bloody Fist Records, 2014)

Dan Sicko – *Techno Rebels* (Bpi Communications, 1999)

Daniel Tecoult, Florian Pittion-Rossillon – *DJ Radium: Le théâtre du bruit* (Signal Zero, 2023)

Disco Pogo – *Aphex Twin: A Disco Pogo Tribute* (Disco Pogo Ltd, 2024)

Ed Gillett – *Party Lines: Dance Music and the Making of Modern Britain* (Picador, 2023)

Felix Denk, Sven von Thülen – *Der Klang Der Familie: Berlin, Techno and the Fall of the Wall* (Books on Demand, 2014)

Frank Owen – *Clubland: The Fabulous Rise and Murderous Fall of Club Culture* (Crown, 2004)

Freek van Kraaikamp – *Drokz Kapot Hard* (Elitepauper Publishers, 2021)

Gert van Veen – *Release / Celebrate Life: The Story of ID&T* (Mary Go Wild, 2017)

Hillegonda C. Rietveld – *This is Our House: House music, cultural spaces and Technologies* (Routledge, 1998)

Judy Wajcman – *Technofeminism* (Polity, 2004)

Laurent Garnier, David Brun-Lambert – *Electrochoc* (Rocket 88, 2015)

Mark Angelo Harrison – *A Darker Electricity: The Origins of the Spiral Tribe Sound System* (Velocity Press, 2023)

Mark Archer – *The Man Behind the Mask* (Music Mondays & Straight Six Publishing, 2016)

Mark van Bergen – *Dutch Dance: How The Netherlands took the lead in Electronic Music*

Culture (Mary Go Wild, 2018)

Matt Anniss – *Join the Future: Bleep Techno & the Birth Of British Bass Music* (Velocity Press, 2019)

Matthew Collin – *Altered State: The Story of Ecstasy Culture and Acid House* (Serpent's Tail, 2009)

Michaelangelo Matos – *The Underground is Massive* (Dey Street Books, 2016)

Murder Channel – *Breakcore Guidebook* (Murder Channel, 2019)

Murder Channel – *Hardcore Techno Guidebook* (Murder Channel, 2021)

Praxis – *Everything Else is Even More Ridiculous* (Molehill Publishing, 2015)

Rebekah Farrugia – *Beyond the Dancefloor* (University of Chicago Press, 2012)

Remko van Bork – *Rotterdam Popstad* (Popunie, 2025)

Richard Russell – *Liberation Through Hearing* (White Rabbit, 2020)

Ronald Tukker – *Rotterdam in the House* (Brave New Books, 2015)

Simon Reynolds – *Generation Ecstasy: Into the World of Techno and Rave Culture* (Routledge, 1998)

Théo Lessour – *Berlin Sampler: From Cabaret to Techno: 1904-2012, a century of Berlin music* (Ollendorff Verlag Berlin, 2009)

Tobias Rapp – *Lost and Sound: Berlin, Techno and the Easyjet Set* (Suhrkamp Verlag, 2012)

Tresor– *Tresor: True Stories* (NOVA MD, 2022)

Uwe Schütte – *Kraftwerk: Future Music from Germany* (Penguin, 2020)

Wayne Anthony – *Class of 88: The True Acid House Experience* (Virgin Books, 1998)

DANCE OR DIE DISCOGRAPHY

1. WE HAVE ARRIVED

1989 Mescalinum United – *Into Mekong Center* (PCP 001)

1990 Freebase Factory – *Born To Go* (PCP 002)

1990 Various – *Frankfurt Trax Vol. 1: House Of Techno* (PCP 004)

1990 Mescalinum United – *Reflections Of 2017* (PCP 006)

1991 Mescalinum United / the Mover – *Planet Core Productions Special AA Side* (IS001)

1991 The Mover – *Frontal Sickness Part 1* (PCP 005)

1991 Al Rakhun Feat. Bunker Youth – *To The Audience* (PCP 011 / Dope on Plastic)

1991 Raw Power Organisation – *1991 (And I Just Begun)* (PCP 013)

1992 Various (feat DJ Dag, Sven Vath, Delirium) – *Frankfurt Trax Volume 2* (Dance Pool)

1992 Friends Of Alex – *What Is..? Fick Dich* (No Mercy Records)

1988 Various – *Techno! The New Dance Sound Of Detroit* (10 Records)

1988 Bigod 20 – *Body & Energize* (ZYX Records)

1988 Off – *Organisation For Fun* (ZYX Records)

1989 Various – *Welcome To The Technodrome* (Techno Drome International)

1991 Second Phase – *Mentasm* (R & S Records)

1992 Aphex Twin – *Didgeridoo* (R & S Records)

1992 Aphex Twin – *Analogue Bubblebath Vol 3* (R & S Records)

1992 Lenny Dee (with Outlander & The Source Experience) – *Untitled* (R & S Records)

2. INDUSTRY DESTROYERS

1987 Members Of The House (feat Banks, Mills) – *Keep Believin'* (Vibe Records)

1990 Final Cut (feat Mills) – *Deep In 2 The Cut* (Big Sex Records)

1990 Underground Resistance w/ Yolanda – *Your Time Is Up* (UR 001)

1990 Underground Resistance – *Sonic EP* (UR 002)

1991 Blake Baxter – *The Prince Of Techno* (UR 006)

1991 The Vision (Hood) – *Gyroscopic EP* (UR 008)
1991 Underground Resistance – *Riot EP* (UR 010)
1991 Underground Resistance – *Fuel For The Fire Attend The Riot* (UR012)
1991 Underground Resistance (Mills) – *Punisher* (UR 017)
1992 Underground Resistance (Banks) – *The Final Frontier* (UR003)
1992 H&M – *Tranquilizer EP* (AX-001)
1992 X-103 – *Thera EP* (AX-003)
1991 X-101 – *X-101* (Tresor 1)
1992 X-102 – *Discovers The Rings Of Saturn* (Tresor 4)
1992 Various – *Auferstanden Aus Ruinen* (Tresor Compilation 1)
1992 Ace The Space – *9 Is A Classic* (Dance Ecstasy 2001)
1992 Smash? – *Smash!* (reissued as *Konstablerwache*) (No Mercy Records)
1993 Various (feat PCP 'Frankfurt Anthem') – *The Judgement Day* (Mayday Comp Vol. III)
1993 Various – *Frankfurt Trax Vol 4: The Hall Of Fame* (Dance Pool)
1993 Jeff Mills – *Waveform Transmission Vol. 1* (Tresor 11)
1994 Robert Hood – *Internal Empire* (Tresor 27)
1994 Leathernecks – *Test Attack* (Kotzaak Unltd.)

3. MAKE SOME FUCKIN NOISE

1990 Altern 8 – *Overload EP* (Network Records)
1991 The Hypnotist – *The Hardcore EP* (Rising High Records)
1991 Earth Leakage Trip – *Psychotronic* (Moving Shadow)
1991 The House Crew – *Keep The Fire Burning / Get On Up* (Production House)
1991 The Prodigy – *What Evil Lurks / Charly* (XL Recordings)
1991 SL2 – *DJ's Take Control / Way In My Brain* (XL Recordings)
1992 Various – *Hardcore DJ's...Take Control* (Perfecto)
1992 Acen – *Trip To The Moon (Part 1, Part 2, Part 3)* (Production House)
1992 Kicks Like A Mule – *The Bouncer* (Tribal Bass Records)
1992 Spiral Tribe – *Breach The Peace* (Big Life)
1992 Spiral Tribe – *Forward The Revolution* (Big Life)
1993 Spiral Tribe – *Spiral Tribe Sound System* (Big Life)

1993 Spiral Tribe – *Tecno Terra* (Big Life)

1993 SP 23 – *Network 23 EP* (Rabbit City Records)

1993 SP 23 / Unit Moebius – *Out Of The Blue* (Blue Attack Records)

1996 69db, Person Unknown, Warlock (written '93) – *Unknown Source* (Network23)

4. VERY FUCKING MENTAL

1991 Aphex Twin – *Analogue Bubblebath Vol 2* (Rabbit City Records)

1992 Scaremonger – *Scaremonger EP* (Praxis 1)

1993 Bourbonese Qualk – *Autonomia* (Praxis 5 CD)

1993 Disciples of Belial – *Songs Of Praise* (Praxis 7)

1994 Various – *Eurobeat 2000 Club Classics Volume One* (Kickin Records)

1995 Neuroviolence – *Shattered EP* (Zero Tolerance Records London)

1995 Lorenz Attractor – *Strange Attractor EP* (Praxis 13)

1995 Disciples of Belial – *Goat Of Mendes EP* (Praxis 17)

1996 Various – *Dead By Dawn* (Praxis 23)

1997 Suicide Squad – *8 Bit Shit* (Industrial Strength Records)

1997 Suicide Squad And Max Death – *Untitled* (Strike Records)

1997 Traffik – *Darkside* (Born To Kill)

1997 Nasenbluten – *Cheapcore EP* (Strike Records)

5. FUCKING HOSTILE

1988 The Original Gangsters of Freestyle – *Get The Hoe* (Underworld Records)

1988 Bonesbreaks – *Hard, Raw & Raunchy Beats For DJ's* (Underworld Records)

1989 Frankie Bones & Lenny Dee – *Looney Tunes Volume One* (Nu Groove Records)

1989 Frankie Bones & Lenny Dee – *Just As Long As I Got You* (XL Recordings)

1989 Various – *Drumdrops Vol. 1 Essential Break Beats & Loops* (Big Break)

Lenny Dee Pop Engineer

1988 Brooklyn Funk Essentials – *Change The Track* (Minimal Records)

1990 The KLF – *What Time Is Love?* (KLF Communications)

1990 New Order – *Confusion* (Factory)

1991 The Shamen – *En-Tact* (One Little Indian)

1993 United Rave States (Carl & Nicky pre DOA) – *Sunrise In Rotterdam* (A & X Records)

1993 Glitch – *Trauma EP* (IS010)

1993 DJ Skinhead – *Fuckin Hostile* (IS017)

1994 Temper Tantrum – *The Uncontrollable Fit EP* (IS023)

1994 Disciples Of Annihilation (DOA) – *Industrial Power '9d4* (IS024)

1994 DJ Skinhead – *Extreme Terror* (IS026)

1994 Strychnine – *The Utopia Project* (IS027)

1994 Ralphie Dee – *Totally Cained* (IS029)

1995 Nasenbluten – *100% No Soul Guaranteed* (IS030)

1995 Delta Nine – *Wehrmacht* (IS031)

1997 Disciples Of Annihilation (DOA) – *New York City Speedcore* (Earache)

6. FIGHTING SPIRIT

1991 Liza N Eliaz – *Initial Gain* (Atomic Records)

1992 Stockhousen – *E-Mission* (Bonzai Records 001)

1994 Pure & Liza N Eliaz – *Killerbees On Acid* (Loop Records)

1995 DJ Dano & Liza N Eliaz – *Energy Boost* (Mokum Records)

1995 Liza N Eliaz – *Romper Stomper Mix* (ISR comp) (Earache)

1995 Liza N Eliaz & LKJ Sisters – *Untitled* (RPG-7)

1998 Liza N Eliaz – *Voyager Loops* (Provision Records)

2001 Liza N Eliaz – *Liza N Eliaz* (Uncivilised World, posthumous anthology)

1995 Loftgroover – *The Scare Core EP* (Redhead Records)

1995 Manu Le Malin – *Paris Hardcore DJ Mix* (ISR comp) (Earache)

1995 Manu Le Malin – *Memory* (IST011)

1996 Loftgroover Presents Zeed / Skrewface – *Scarecore II EP* (Redhead Records)

1997 Manu Le Malin – *Biomechanik Vol 1* (F Communications)

1998 Loftgroover – *Loftgroover Presents Speedcore* (Harmless)

1999 Manu Le Malin – *Biomechanik Vol 2* (F Communications)

2002 Manu Le Malin – *Fighting Spirit* (Bloc 46)

2005 Manu Le Malin – *Biomechanik III: The Final Chapter* (F Communications)

7. BE A FREAK, BE YOU

1989 Fierce Ruling Diva – *I Don't Wanna Be A Freak* (LES 001)

1990 2001 – *The Sound Of Planet Earth: Amsterdam's Most Talented Vol. 1* (LES 003)

1990 Fierce Ruling Diva Featuring DJ Dano & Myrna Shakison – *Floorfiller* (LES 007)

1991 Fierce Ruling Diva – *Housenation* (12" entry to Rotterdam party) (HN91)

1992 Various – *Forever Underground Subtopia* (LES CD2)

1988 Hithouse – *Jack To The Sound Of The Underground* (ARS Benelux)

1989 Silver Bullet – *20 Seconds To Comply* (Tam Tam Records)

1990 Holy Noise – *Father Forgive Them* (Hithouse Records)

1991 Nebula II – *Seance / Atheama* (Reinforced Records)

1991 Free Base International – *The FBI Futureworld EP* (Planet Core Productions)

1991 Holy Noise Feat the Global Insert Project – *James Brown Is Still Alive!!* (Hithouse)

1991 Speedy J – *Face The Future EP* ('Pull Over' bonus) (Stealth Records)

1991 Ricky the Dragon "Posse" – *It's Techno Time EP* (Stealth Records)

1992 The Ultimate Seduction – *The Ultimate Seduction* (Interdance Records)

1992 Cybersonik – *Thrash* (Plus 8)

8. HARD SCORE

1992 Euromasters – *Amsterdam Waar Lech Dat Dan?* (ROT 001)

1992 DJ Rob – *1992 Is For You* (ROT 003)

1992 Rotterdam Termination Source – *Poing* (ROT 004)

1992 Sperminator – *No Women Allowed* (ROT 008)

1992 Euromasters – *Alles Naar De Kl--te* (ROT 009)

1992 General Noise – *Rotterdam Subway* (ROT 010)

1993 Bald Terror – *Rotterdam* (ROT 018)

1993 Euromasters – *Oranje Boven* (ROT 121)

1994 Euromasters – *Hardscore* (ROT 035)

9. HAPPY, BOUNCY, MENTAL

1995 DJ Paul – *Luv U More / Rainbow In The Sky* (Rotterdam Records)

1996 DJ Paul – *Rave On / The Promised Land* (Rotterdam Records)

1995 Technohead – *I Wanna Be A Hippy* (feat Flamman & Abraxas Radio Mix) (Mokum)

1995 Party Animals – *Have You Ever Been Mellow?* (Mokum Records)

1996 Party Animals – *Aquarius* (Mokum Records)

1996 Hakkûhbar – *Gabbertje* (Roadrunner Records)

1993 Undercover Anarchist – *Kingdom* (Ruffneck Records)

1994 DJ Paul Presents the Forze DJ Team – *May The Forze Be With You* (FORZE 1)

1994 Waxweazle – *Going Down Again* (Waxweazle / ID&T Music)

1994 Rob Gee – *Gabber Up Your Ass* (Industrial Strength Records)

1994 Q-Tex – *Equazion Remix EP* (Evolution Records)

1994 Various – *Hardcore Hell* (Evolution Records CD001)

1995 Various – *Bouncy Techno Anthems compilation* (*M8* mag curated) (Rogue Trooper)

1995 Scott Brown Meets Paul Elstak – *Feel The Music* (FORZE 3)

1995 Scott Brown – *Do What Ya Like! (The Rezerection Anthem)* (Evolution Records)

1996 Scott Brown – *The Theory Of Evolution* (Evolution Records)

10. TERRORCORE

1992 The Speed Freak – *The Speed Freak* (Mono Tone)

1992 Tanith – *T2 EP* (BASH 004)

1993 Xol Dog 400 – *Sons Of T2* (KM-Musik)

1994 Stickhead – *Slaughterhouse EP* (Kotzaak Unltd.)

1995 Stickhead – *World's Hardest Kotzaak* (Kotzaak Unltd.)

1995 Nordcore GMBH – *Hartcore City Downtown* (Nordcore Records NORD 1)

1996 Boogle (Beagle, misspelt) & Bullfrog – *Hard Life* (WAR-1)

1993 The Dreamteam – *Thunderdome* (ID&T Music)

1995 Various – *Terrordrome VI: Welcome To Planet Hardcore* (Control)

1996 Various – *DochSchon EP* (Gabba Nation Records 01)

1996 Various – *Bunker Beats One* (BMG)

1996 DJ Lady Dana – *Heroes Of Hardcore DJ Mix* (Arcade, ID&T)

1996 Various – *We Are One Family: Love Parade Compilation* (Low Spirit Recordings)

1996 Various – *Thunderdome '96: Dance Or Die!* (Arcade, ID&T)

2005 Various – *Tresor Vol. 13 It's Not Over* (Tresor Records)

11. THE FINAL THUNDERCLAP

1998 Promo – *Dancefloor Hardcore / Metal Warfare* (Promo File 001 & 002 / ID&T)

2001 Promo – *Escape From The Hostile / Rude Awakening* (Promo File 010/ A & B / ID&T)

2001 Various – *Just Fuck, Not Love!!!* (Limited Fuckparade Edition) (Cunt Records)

2004 Dana – *Restyled / Back In Time* (Danamite)

2011 Peckerhead – *Gabbertje EP* (Headache Rekords)

2012 Various – *Thunderdome: The Final Exam 20 Years Of Hardcore* (Be Yourself Music)

2017 Peckerhead – *Copenhagen Bloodbank* (Mokum Records)

2021 Peckerhead – *Not A Normal Day Since 1992* (Peckerhead Industries)

2023 Peckerhead – *Dreams & Doubts* (Mokum Records)

12. NEO-RAVE ARMAGEDDON

1990 The Ragga Twins – *Ragga Trip / Hooligan 69* (Shut Up And Dance Records)

1992 Altern 8 – *Full On Mask Hysteria* (Network Records)

1996 Squarepusher – *Feed Me Weird Things* (Rephlex)

1996 Diplomat – *Cool And Deadly* (Deathchant 04)

1997 µ-Ziq – *Lunatic Harness* (Planet Mu / Virgin)

1997 Various – *Mealtime* (Planet Mu)

1998 Hellfish & Producer – *No More Rock N Roll* (DEATHCHANT 16)

1999 Hellfish – *Turntable Savage* (DEATHCHANT 24)

2001 Hellfish – *Meat Machine Broadcast System* (Planet Mu)

2004 Various – *Now That's What I Call Wrong Music Volume 1* (Wrong Music)

2004 Shitmat – *Killababylonkutz* (Planet Mu)

2004 Various Artists – *Amµnition* (Planet Mu)

2005 Venetian Snares – *Rossz Csillag Alatt Született* (Planet Mu)

2005 DJ Scotch Egg – *Scotch Chicken / Scotch Party* (Wrong Music)

2006 Ebola – *Reflective Shots* (Wrong Music)

2007 Ceephax – *Volume One* (Rephlex)

2013 Various – *Bang Face Neo-Rave Armageddon* (Bang Face BF001)

2015 Squarepusher – *Damogen Furies* (Warp)

13. PHUTURE GABBERS

1993 The Mover – *The Final Sickness* (Planet Core Productions)

1994 The Mover & Rave Creator – *Rave The Planet* (Cold Rush Records)

1995 Inferno Brothers – *Slaves To The Rave* (Dance Ecstasy 2001)

1996 Lenny Dee & The Hardcore Warriors – *Funky Twisted* (Industrial Strength Limited)

1997 Marc Acardipane – *Best Of 1989-1997* (LP) (ID&T)

2002 The Mover – *Frontal Frustration* (Tresor)

2017 The Outside Agency – *Blue Stories* (Heresy)

2017 Various – *Inutile De Fuir* (Casual Gabberz Records 001)

2018 The Mover - *Undetected Act From The Gloom Chamber* (Planet Phuture)

2018 Paul Seul – *Entretenir Surveiller Sécuriser* (Casual Gabberz Records 004)

2020 Kilbourne – *Pillsurfer* (Casual Gabberz Records 012)

2020 Ascendant Vierge – *Influenceur* (Live From Earth Klub)

2020 Various – *United Ravers Against Fascism* (Live From Earth Klub / Never Sleep)

2023 Various – *Meilleurs Vœux (Forever)* (Casual Gabberz Records)

14. GOD IS A GBBRGRRL

2017 Somniac One – *Troubled Youth EP* (PRSPCT XTRM)

2019 Somniac One – *Safety Bangers For The New Generation* (PRSPCT XTRM)

2019 Kilbourne – *NJ Terror* (Industrial Strength Records)

2023 Kilbourne – *Milkshake* (PRSPCT)

2023 Various – *The World Blurs* (Explity Music)

2024 KimberlaID – *The Time Has Come* (Explity Music)

2024 Somniac One – *To All My Soggy Creatures Of The Night* (Somniverse)

2025 Kilbourne – *If Not To Give A Fantasy* (Hammerhead Records)

OUTRO: JOIN A CVLT!

1992 Secret Squirrel – *The Magic Flute EP* (Bogwoppa Records)

2002 Baseck – *US Tour Mix* (self-release CD-r)

2005 DJ Hidden / Limewax – *The Resonators / Pain* (PRSPCT 001)

2015 Dolphin – *The Polychronican / Raiders Cap* (PRSPCT XTRM)

2020 The DJ Producer – *Doomsday Expanded Redux* (Rebelscum)

2020 Dolphin – *Ebbs & Flows* (PRSPCT)

2022 Slave to Society – *Distorted Thoughts EP* (self-release)

2023 Slave to Society – *Abstract Venom EP* (PRSPCT)

2023 Neurocore – *Existences* (PRSPCT)

2024 RaBBeAT – *Insignificant Waveforms* (PRSPCT)

2024 Thrasher – *Rotterdam Hardcore EP* (DEATHCHANT 110)

SPECIAL THANKS TO EVERYONE WHO PRE-ORDERED THE BOOK

69db, Pascal Adam, Erki Aun, Timur Azizov, Ollie Badger, Sophie Balch, Zsolt Bangha, Stephen Banks, Lily Beckett, Klaudia Biedzio, David Brownlie, Michael A Buick, Barry Bullas, Caroline Burnett, Samantha Burt, Andrew Bush, Diego Canneto, Laima Cavalera, Holly Cheek, Victoria Chhim, Amardeep Chima, Rob Christensen, Alexia Chuck, Luke Coleman, Charlotte Colgate, Thomas Crawford, Issy Croker, Dave Curran, Thomas DeBellis, Diane Delallée, Linda Dicker, Malgorzata Duszczyk, Victor Evans, Ben Fewster, Johan Jacobsson Franzén, Stephanie Gibson, Julia Gilman, Kevin Gilmour, Baptiste Heiles, Emily Helms, Johan Herzelius, Sunniva Hestenes, Robert Hogg, Nick Hoppezak, Charlie Hunk, Peter Irvine, Francis Jaques, Mark Jermyn, Mandy Johnston, Alexander Kassberg, Daniel Kirby, Koen Koopmans, Neil Moore, Andrew Nesbit, Tosh Ohta, Richard Oldfield, Paul Keay, Ashe Kilbourne, Patricia Koekkoek, Paul Lakwijk, Marja Lammers, Richard Lawson, Tim Lee, Jonathan Livingstone, Angel Martinez, Robin Smeds Mattila, Ray McLaughlin, Kevin Mcpherson, Jason Mendonca, Morgan Meriguet, David Milloy, Andrea Molteni, Joe Morrison, Janine Neuf, Wladimir Nicolaas, Christian Olofsson, Raymond Oosterbaan, Athanasios Papapadopoulos, Jamie Pearson, Nicola Perrow, Maddy Quail, Mark Quail, Nicola Ranger, Daniel Rønhave, Samuel Russell, Justin Santana, Julio Santo Domingo, Andrew Seal, Fedor Shutov, Peri Siolis (aka GLOWKiD), Anita Spijker, Olivia Stearn, Craig Stedman, Joris Strijbos, Sergey Surganov, Michael Tolan, Anne-Marie Travers, John Trevains, Amy Van-Baaren, Bart Van Bokhoven, Sietse van Daalen, Jelle Van Leeuwen, Maurice van de Berkt, Jill van Put, Dennis van Rijswijk, Alexander Waldron, Hayley Walker, Joe Walker, Sebastian Weber, Thom Wilkins, Aiden Witt, DJ WOO, Georgy Zhukov, Stefan ZMK

ALSO AVAILABLE ON VELOCITY PRESS

OUT OF SPACE - JIM OTTEWILL

Jim Ottewill's exploration of UK club culture and the urban landscapes that have housed it returns in a newly remixed form. This extended version features a new chapter exploring hidden histories and untold stories within Birmingham's nocturnal scene to provide more insights into the past, present and future of electronic music culture.

"As gentrification, lack of funding, stifling politics and the pandemic continue to pummel nightlife, it feels all the more poignant to chart the past and present of raving, while questioning what's next. With lively and forensic research, clarity of thought and a passion for keeping clubbing's resilient spirit alive, Out of Space is less of a commemoration and more of a rallying cry." The Face

"Ottewill's book is tireless in its seeking out of new buzzes in grassroots clubland, LGBT collectives and local scenes, all of them ensuring euphoric highs for future generations of ravers." The Wire

velocitypress.uk/product/out-of-space-book

ALSO AVAILABLE ON VELOCITY PRESS

JOIN THE FUTURE - MATT ANNISS

Matt Anniss's critically acclaimed alternative history of UK dance music in the acid house era returns in updated and expanded form. Named by Rolling Stone UK as one of the best books on British music culture, *Join The Future* puts forward a persuasive new argument about the origins of UK club culture's long-running love affair with bass.

A mixture of social, cultural, musical and oral history based on five years of research and hundreds of interviews, *Join The Future* tells the previously hidden history of 'bleep' for the first time. It brings forth the untold stories of bleep's pioneers and those that came in their wake, moving from mid-80s electro all-dayers and reggae soundsystem clashes in the North and Midlands, to the birth of breakbeat hardcore and jungle in London and the South East in the early '90s.

Now expanded to include more interviews, analysis and a brand-new 'afterword' chapter, *Join The Future* is one of the most revealing and significant books on dance music in years.

"A significant contribution to the canon of dance music literature" – Matthew Collin, author of *Altered State* and *Rave on*

'Brings to the surface a hidden cultural history and a scene that reverberated around the world' Lanre Bakare

velocitypress.uk/product/join-the-future-book

ALSO AVAILABLE ON VELOCITY PRESS

THE RADIO PHONICS LABORATORY - JUSTIN PATRICK MOORE

The Radio Phonics Laboratory explores the intersection of technology and creativity that shaped the sonic landscape of the 20th century. This fascinating story unravels the intricate threads of telecommunications, from the invention of the telephone to the advent of global communication networks.

At the heart of the narrative is the evolution of speech synthesis, a groundbreaking innovation that not only revolutionized telecommunications but also birthed a new era in electronic music. Tracing the origins of synthetic speech and its applications in various fields, the book unveils the pivotal role it played in shaping the artistic vision of musicians and sound pioneers.

"From telegraphy to the airwaves, by way of Hedy Lamarr and Doctor Who, listening to Hal 9000 sing to us whilst a Clockwork Orange unravels the past and present, Moore spirits us on an expansive trip across the twentieth century of sonic discovery. The joys of electrical discovery are unravelled page by page." Robin Rimbaud aka Scanner

"In this captivating exploration of electronic music, Justin Patrick Moore unveils its evolution as guided by telecommunication technology, spotlighting the enigmatic laboratories of early experimenters who shaped the sound of 20th century music. A must-read for electronic musicians & sound artists alike." Kim Cascone

velocitypress.uk/product/radio-phonics-laboratory-book

ALSO AVAILABLE ON VELOCITY PRESS

A DARKER ELECTRICITY - MARK ANGELO HARRISON

At the time, it was unclear why the UK government targeted the Spiral Tribe travelling sound system. Even after arresting many key members and launching one of Britain's biggest court cases against them. Was it really because they were a marauding horde of anarcho-techno-pirates, their outlandish music calling a generation to rebel against conservatism, convention, and even consensus reality?

Or was it because, as pioneers of the 1990s free party movement, championing the new British breakbeat and European techno sound, they were reclaiming social space in warehouses and out under the stars? Each weekend, they pulled ever bigger crowds away from consumer culture. No superstar DJs, no door policy and everyone dancing together as equals. An inspiring, unifying force of creativity.

As Spiral Tribe's co-founder and visual artist, Mark Angelo Harrison has a unique perspective to tell their inside story. He vividly charts their nomadic journey and the rapid escalation of their popularity - and notoriety.

"A rip-roaring modern-day adventure story and an odyssey about following your dreams. Mark Angelo Harrison's razor-sharp narrative makes the words zing on the page." Chris Liberator (Liberator/Stay Up Forever)

ALSO AVAILABLE ON VELOCITY PRESS

DREAMING IN YELLOW - HARRY HARRISON

Emerging from Nottingham in the summer of 1989, the DiY Collective were one of the first house sound systems in the UK. Merging the anarchic lineage of the free festival scene, the cultural and political anger of bands like Crass with the new, irresistible electronic pulse of acid house, they bridged the idealistic void left by the moral implosion of the commercial rave scene.

Written by Harry Harrison, one of DiY's founding members, this book traces their origins back to early formative experiences, describing in detail the seminal clubs, parties, festivals and records that forged the collective. Dreaming in Yellow is an attempt to distil the story of DiY's tumultuous existence and the remarkably eclectic, outrageous and occasionally deranged story of them doing it themselves.

"Full of wild tales from the highest of times, this is the story of an intrepid crew of idealistic hedonists whose quest for freedom and joy created some of the peak moments of Britain's rave counterculture." Matthew Collin (author of *Altered State* and *Rave On*)

ALSO AVAILABLE ON VELOCITY PRESS

TAKE NO PRISONERS - KEITH ROBINSON

Keith Robinson was the founding member of Desert Storm, a sound system that hosted free parties across the UK and Europe in the 90s. Known as Keef to his friends, he was renowned for his military precision in organising illicit raves and infused the scene with a socially conscious ethos.

His first forays into party organising in Glasgow led to tours of the UK and the emerging European teknival movement, political activism for events such as Reclaim The Streets in Trafalgar Square, and even humanitarian aid missions to war-torn Bosnia during the Balkans conflict. Keef's life took an unexpected turn in 2007 when he joined the army and served in Afghanistan, where he wrote most of this candid and thrilling autobiography.

However, tragically, in 2016, his life ended in the River Thames, leaving his story unfinished. It's taken almost ten years – and lots of hurdles to overcome – to finally bring Keef's story to the world.

"Keith was one of the most remarkable and inspiring characters in UK rave culture history – an intrepid motivator who led a thrilling life to a heartbreaking conclusion." Matthew Collin (author of *Dream Machines*, *Rave On* and *Altered State*)

velocitypress.uk/product/take-no-prisoners-book/